COACHING THE TEAM

by

Tony Waiters

World of Soccer
Vancouver

THE WORLD OF SOCCER "COACHING" SERIES

Coaching 6, 7 & 8 Year Olds — Tony Waiters and Bobby Howe

Coaching 9, 10 & 11 Year Olds — Bobby Howe and Tony Waiters

Coaching The Team — Tony Waiters

Coaching The Team Player — Bobby Howe

Coaching The Goalkeeper — Tony Waiters

Teaching Offside — Bob Evans and Tony Waiters

Soccer Is Fun — A Workbook for 6, 7 & 8 Year Olds

Micro Soccer — Rules And Regulations

Great Games For Soccer — Billy McNicol

First published January 15th, 1990, by WORLD OF SOCCER
5880 Falcon Road, West Vancouver, British Columbia

(604) 921-8963

First printing January, 1990
Second printing September, 1991

CREDITS

Editor: Bob Dunn
Illustrator: Martin Nichols
Copy Processing: Barbara Schiffner
Layout and Design: Dunn Communications Ltd.

Manufactured by Hemlock Printers Ltd.

ACKNOWLEDGEMENTS

Allan Brown
Allen Wade
Burnley FC

This book is written for all the soccer coaches of the world who have the daunting task of helping bring together a collection of individuals into a single unit — The Team — playing the world's greatest game.

DEDICATION

To the memory of my Mom and Dad, who never stopped encouraging their two soccer children.

TABLE OF CONTENTS

THE WORLD'S GREATEST GAME

The Team Coach 6
Objectives of Manual 7
Age Considerations 8
Individual Skill vs Team Play 10
Psychological and Physiological 11

DEPLOYMENT OF PLAYERS

Systems of Play 12
Attacking Support 13
Defensive Support 13
Offside 14
Width of Field 15
Team Shape 16
Thirds of the Field 20

PRACTISE SECTION

The Game is the Teacher 24
Presentation of Practises 24

The Practises – Part I. Team Games

5 vs 2 26
The Numbers Game 28
Noah's Lark 28
Micro Soccer 30
4-a-side 32
Zone Game 34
Chip 'n Dale 36

The Practises – Part II. Shadow Play

Introduction 40
Introducing it to the Team 42
Methodology 43
With Larger Numbers 44
Two Team Shadow 46
Further Options 47
Postscript 47

The Practises – Part III. Larger Numbers

Crossroads 50
Big Shot 52
4-Goal Game 54
The Man Marking Game 56
5-a-side 58
Attack vs Defense 60
Mixed Bag 62
Super 8's 64
Full Field Team Games 66
11-a-side 67
Many Ways Up Everest 67

APPENDIX

The Goalkeeper's Team Role 69
Factors in Team Development 70
Coach's Questionnaire 71
Sample Session Plan for U-16 Team 72

THE WORLD'S GREATEST TEAM GAME

The names of Pele, Maradona and Bobby Charlton are synonymous with the best there is in soccer. The fact is, they may never have been heard of had these players not been members of a team. Jack Nicklaus, Muhammad Ali, Jimmy Connors take their place in the World Sports Hall of Fame forever, because of their individual accomplishments in golf, boxing and tennis, respectively.

Soccer is not a 1 vs 1 game. It is 11 vs 11. It is a team game. Of course, one player can make a significant difference in the team performance — positively or negatively. But how many teams succeed when they find themselves a player short? In soccer, 11 vs 10 is not a fair soccer match-up.

Pele, Maradona and Bobby Charlton, in their prime, would have had little or no chance of beating a team of 11 average adult players. Eleven vs 3 — no matter how talented the three — is no contest. That is why in the final analysis, team play will be of paramount importance.

The greatest test for the soccer coach is to bring individuals together in order to maximize their abilities for the benefit of the team performance. The coach must also minimize individual weaknesses through team strategy and through the co-operation of teammates compensating for and complementing one another.

"The team performance should always be greater than the sum of the individual parts."

The Team Coach

Any coach involved with a team at any level of soccer knows the joy of success — of seeing the team play well — and the despair of sub-standard performance. The fact is, for every winner there has to be a loser. Everybody is happy when the team is playing well. Many wonder if a coach is needed! But when things go wrong, everyone — players, parents, fans and friends — look to the coach FOR HELP!

As a coach for 30 years, I've had the privilege of coaching teams of top professionals — championship teams in Europe and North America. I've coached a team of 13 year olds in British Columbia, Canada, and a team at the same age level in Lancashire, England. I've had some great times — and not-so-great times!

As the years go on, I've learned from hard experience it is better for everyone associated with a team, including the coach, to produce more successes than failures.

This book does not bring any guarantees. There is no "money back" if your team fails to perform. What this book does bring is some tried and trusted practise methods that work and that,when properly applied, bring far more joy than despair.

OBJECTIVES OF MANUAL

The objectives of this manual are simple:

To help coaches of youth soccer teams set up practises that are enjoyable yet greatly assist in improving the collective team performance.

Too often at practise, players are put through a series of drills and games that are mainly technique oriented, culminating in a "free" scrimmage. In many cases the practises are good — but usually fail to address the problem of players combining together as an effective group.

Why is "Team" Practise Neglected by Coaches?

Putting on practise sessions that bring the whole of the group together with one common purpose — often using only one ball — is not easy. The complications of numbers; the difficulty of analysis; the fact that all players are sharing one ball thus reducing the number of kicks per player — all these factors mitigate against running "team practises" as opposed to small group situations.

Recognizing the difficulties, this manual has been written specifically with the "team" in mind. It is not the definitive soccer book of all tactical systems and methods. The aim is to give you, the coach, practises that work and help maximize the team performance.

Coaches Can't Leave "Team Play" to Chance

The development of team play and team strategy is often left to chance — or to chalk talks and half-time and full-time "bawl outs" (usually less productive than chance!).

Getting 11 (or 6 or 5) players to work together will always produce less than perfect results. In the practise session, sharing a ball between 12 or 16 is not going to give as many ball contacts per player as it would with a group of 2 or 3 — and the fun factor must always be considered.

"Fault Analysis" by the coach is far more difficult with a situation complicated by numbers. It's much easier to see what is going on in a 2 vs 1 situation than in 7 vs 7.

Consequently, there is a real temptation to keep practises uncomplicated — particularly in terms of numbers — with a scrimmage at the end. While there may not be anything particularly wrong with this — especially for 6 to 12 year olds — as players move into competitive 11-a-side play, avoiding "the team concept" in the practise session would be a mistake.

One old pro used to say to me, as we ran our mandatory eight laps of the soccer field at the beginning of practise, watched by the trainer, stop watch in hand: "You don't practise snooker [pool] by running round the table!"

Nor do you develop team play by only playing 2 vs 1.

AGE CONSIDERATIONS

6, 7 and 8 Year Olds — THE BEGINNER PLAYER

Fun and activity are the key considerations at this age. Development of the basic skills — kicking, passing, dribbling, ball control, basic goalkeeping should be presented in fun small-sided games and situations.

9, 10 and 11 Year Olds — THE GOLDEN AGE OF LEARNING

Heavy emphasis on skills development, particularly in situations that allow co-operation with two or three friends. Small-sided practises or games are the principal development vehicles.

12 – 15 Year Olds — EARLY TEENS

The gang concept (peer pressure) becomes one of the most important considerations. Competing with one another and against one another is a key factor in the organization of practise. This is the age when "Team Play" becomes much more important.

16 – 30 Year Olds — THE MATURE AND MATURING PLAYER

Tactics, team work, fitness, strength, individual ability — they must all come together for what are the optimum soccer years in terms of performances. This is the time when strategically-organized set plays assume great importance, and players are better prepared mentally to take the time necessary to make the plan work. Winning (and losing) are very important.

30+ Year Olds — MASTERS SOCCER

Soccer has become "a game for life", and Masters Soccer is becoming much more organized in terms of leagues and tournaments. Even greater emphasis is needed at this time regarding tactics and team play. As the legs begin to fail, the "head" must take over. Experience and know-how are the keys.

Relative to "Team" Practise

Beginner Player: 6, 7 & 8

Average length of practise session — 40 minutes

Techniques:	Learning how to kick and dribble
Skill:	Fun practises mainly involving two co-operating players
Team:	Small-sided games, 2 vs 2 and 3 vs 3
Fitness:	Not a consideration at this age
Free Play:	Very important — preferably 3 vs 3 (supervised but not coached)

Practise Time:	Technique	15%	Skill	15%	Team	25%
	Fitness	0%	Free Play	45%		

Golden Age Player: 9, 10 & 11

Average length of practise session — 60 minutes

Techniques:	Passing, shooting, ball control, 1 vs 1 work, basics of game
Skill:	3 vs 1; 5 vs 2; skill games
Team:	3 vs 3; 4 vs 4 — emphasis on passing and support
Fitness:	Warm-up, introduction to stretching
Free Play:	4 vs 4, 5 vs 5, 6 vs 6 (supervised but not coached)

Practise Time:	Technique	15%	Skill	20%	Team	25%
	Fitness	5%	Free Play	35%		

The Gang: 12 – 15

Average length of practise session — 75 minutes

Techniques:	Crossing, heading, shooting, ball control, 1 vs 1 defending, goalkeeping
Skill:	Heading with opposition; practises that include opposition are important
Team:	Shadow Play, Attack vs Defense (see manual for other practises)
Fitness:	Intensive but short; warm-up important
Free Play:	Do not neglect to include this opportunity in every practise session

Practise Time:	Technique	10%	Skill	20%	Team	30%
	Fitness	15%	Free Play	25%		

The Maturing & Mature Player: 16 – 30

Average length of practise session — 90 minutes

Techniques:	Continued servicing of technique development plus adding the subtleties and finesse, e.g., bending passes, chip passes
Skill:	4 vs 2, 5 vs 2; crossing/shooting/heading work with opposition; passing and control always important
Team:	Much greater emphasis on re-starts — corners, free kicks, etc.; collective defending and attacking work; Shadow Play
Fitness:	Comprehensive and intensive approach to soccer fitness work (highest percentage of time spent on fitness in pre-season and early-season period)
Free Play:	Will always be an essential ingredient of the practise session time

Practise Time:	Technique 10%	Skill	20%	Team	30%
	Free Play 20%	Fitness	20% (more at start of season)		

Please note: While there may not be significant increases or decreases in the percentage of time given to different aspects of the practise session, there is an appreciable difference in actual time, according to age group. For example, 25% of a practise session of 40 minutes devoted to team play for 6, 7 and 8 year olds equals 10 minutes; while 30% of a 90-minute session for mature players equals 27 minutes.

Individual Skill vs Team Play

When does individual development end and team play begin? In the quest to maximize abilities and minimize weaknesses, both in team-play and positional-play coaches have to accept individual weaknesses as well as strengths.

Team play begins as soon as two youngsters co-operate. Two five year olds ganging up to keep a soccer ball from their third "friend" form a team. Maybe not a very nice team — but a team nevertheless!

Positional play, e.g., functioning as a player in a set position or role, such as a goalkeeper, winger, or striker, should not begin until 11-a-side is the regular game. Ideally this should be no earlier than 12 years of age. Teenage players should not be labelled "central defenders" or "right midfielders" once and for all. Players should be allowed to develop their all-round abilities, and to try different positions as they continue to develop their individual skills.

Positions should not be firmly established until 18 years and older. Only the goalkeeper presents a slightly different consideration.

Individual skill development in soccer never ends. My left foot kicking is more skilful today than it ever was. I daren't tell you how long I've been practising!

However, the "Ages of Soccer" as we have pointed out in previous instructional manuals, and in this one, produce particular considerations.

Psychological and Physiological

Youth coaches must regard their young charges as individuals — even though the team concept is becoming increasingly important among teenage players.

Although we may have categorized the 12 – 15 age group as young adolescents, it is impossible to generalize. Some 14 year olds are already well muscled, physically advanced, while others are not much different than the average 11 year old. For many, there is a rapid growth spurt. Some appear to be growing taller by the hour.

The early teens are often turbulent years, punctuated by periods of physical and mental change. Individuals need understanding — and time — to enable them to adjust.

As coaches, we must understand that care must be taken not to over-extend limbs and joints that are going through a major growth period.

Most of all, we must try to understand that for many, the early teens are a time to question (even resent) authority. "Authority" presents itself in the form of parent, teacher, policeman — coach! The kids relate to each other more readily than to figures of authority. They like to "gang around" and to challenge others. This somewhat aggressive and, at times, erratic behaviour can become a positive influence in soccer through skilful handling by the coach.

The characteristics of "Flight and Fight" are as much a part of the game of soccer as they are the psyche of the teenager.

Coaches should organize team activities that give the young players the opportunity to compete and to express themselves physically. The coach should moderate his/her manner where necessary — without losing control and, therefore, respect.

By using the practises recommended in this manual, the players will be able to express themselves physically while driving out some of the inhibitions and hang-ups of adolescence.

Just as importantly, the practises will help players develop themselves as individuals within the team framework.

The Aims of the Manual

1. To outline practises for developing and improving team play — practises that work.

2. To show how to organize these practises within the overall training program.

3. To highlight the key considerations in team coaching — and show how they should be implemented.

This is a practical manual dealing with the realities of the soccer coach — the realities of COACHING THE TEAM.

DEPLOYMENT OF PLAYERS

Systems of Play

The most frequently asked question I field from coaches is this: "What is the best system of play?" They want to know if 4-2-4 is superior to 4-4-2. Does a 4-3-3 have advantages over a 1-4-3-2 system?

The inquiring coaches are usually disappointed with my answer. I point out that different teams use different systems. Zonal defense, man-marking systems with a sweeper, and all the numerical combinations mentioned in the first paragraph have been employed in different ways by different world championship teams. Obviously, there is not one system that is better than all others.

However, all the successful soccer teams of the world do observe certain common principles of team play — in spite of varying number combinations — and we will look at the more important principles in a moment.

Other factors beyond what is best for your **own team** affect the deployment of your own players. For instance, in a game between teams of similar ability, if one team was to play 4 players forward it would be a gamble for the opposing team to play only 2 rear defenders. Most teams would feel compelled to have at least equal numbers of defenders to combat opposing attackers. So common sense adjustments may have to be made even after preparing the game plan. However, it is important that teams do not make too many concessions to the opposition, otherwise a team will never develop its own style of play and strategy.

Supporting Play

Supporting play, both in attack and defense, is the cornerstone of team play. It is the single most important principle of team play. The game is played in triangles and the support shown in the illustration identifies the three main types of attacking support given to the player with the ball.

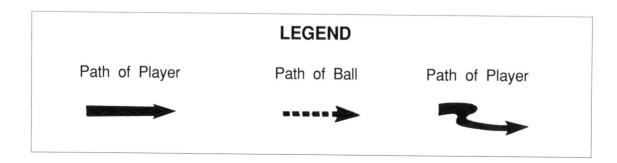

LEGEND		
Path of Player	Path of Ball	Path of Player

Attacking Support

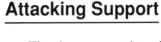

The three supporting players present four options which should be considered in order of priority:

1. Playing the ball forward.

2. Running the ball forward (dribbling), secure in the knowledge there is a rear supporting player covering should the ball be lost.

3. Playing the ball to the side supporting player.

4. Playing the ball backwards.

Please note in the case of the "side support," it is normally better to play the ball forward for the side supporting player to run onto, rather than playing the ball "square." Caution must be exercised with passes to the side supporting player because of the danger of losing the ball, and then being caught by a counter-attack.

FORWARD SUPPORT

SIDE SUPPORT

REAR SUPPORT

DIRECTION OF ATTACK

The distances between players in Attacking Support are usually greater than Defensive Support positions. A distance of 10 – 15 yards in Attacking Support is a good guide as opposed to 5 – 10 yards in Defensive Support. Attacking teams want to open up the space, while the defending teams strive to reduce the space available for the opposition.

Defensive Support

The forward defender plays a mainly passive defensive role — in discouraging a ball played back by the opposition, as well as forcing an opponent to stay in a marking position behind the ball.

However, the forward defender may be required to move "goal-side" of the ball if teammates are outnumbered, or if a rear opposing player makes a forward run (this type of defensive run by the forward defender is known as "tracking").

The rear support defender covers the teammate pressuring the attacker with the ball. Notice that even the "side support" defender is a little deeper than "square" to the player with the ball — and may have to drop deeper if the rear support defender becomes stretched between "covering" and "marking."

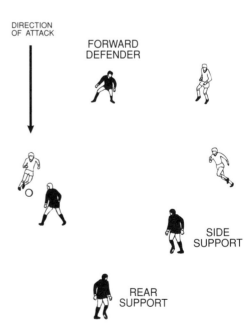

DIRECTION OF ATTACK

FORWARD DEFENDER

SIDE SUPPORT

REAR SUPPORT

Offside

Although "Offside" is not a principle of team play, the Offside Law (Law 11) is perhaps the most important and far-reaching one in terms of team play and team strategy.

It is essential for coaches to have a full knowledge of the offside rule, its interpretation and implementation. In the booklet "Teaching Offside," United States Soccer Federation National Referee Instructor Bob Evans and I have examined the law, its interpretation, how it should be taught to players and its tactical application. If you are not absolutely sure of the complexities of offside, I strongly recommend reading the booklet or acquiring other manuals containing this essential information.

The fact is the referee and the linesmen have total responsibility for applying the offside rule. Coaches who base their team strategy on the decisions of people outside their own organization (i.e., the referee and linesmen) will soon find themselves in trouble.

If taken advantage of, the offside rule does offer some protection to teams and does assist in developing supporting play.

The protection offered by the offside encourages the best teams of the world to push up in support

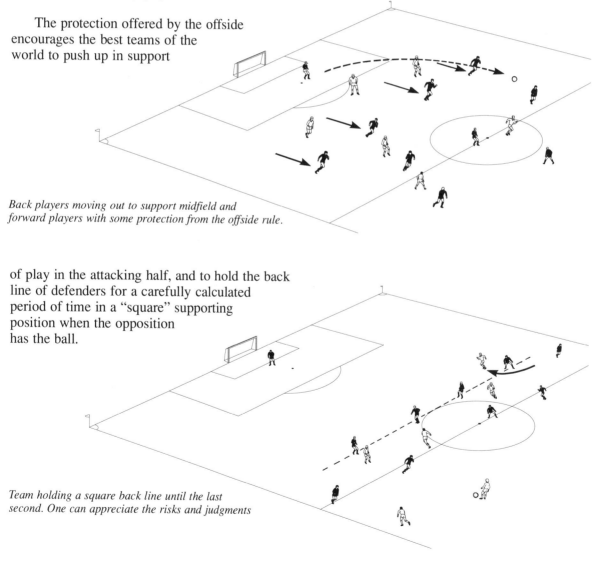

Back players moving out to support midfield and forward players with some protection from the offside rule.

of play in the attacking half, and to hold the back line of defenders for a carefully calculated period of time in a "square" supporting position when the opposition has the ball.

Team holding a square back line until the last second. One can appreciate the risks and judgments

This is perhaps the only situation in the game of soccer where support is deliberately held "square" — and this tactic is not without risks. The play requires first-class understanding by teammates and the knowledge that a referee may or may not call offside — even when the players think the referee should. The referee alone makes the offside call (with or without the assistance of his linesmen). It won't do much good to dispute that decision after the fact. It will be too late.

Width of the Field

Systems of play will determine whether wingers are positioned on the flanks (e.g., 4-2-4) or whether other players eventually move into the flank spaces during the flow of the game (e.g., 4-4-2). Irrespective of the numerical arrangement, all good teams will exploit the use of the width of the field in their attacking play.

Because defenders want to stay together, concentrated and compacted, and because defenders are reluctant to be drawn out of central defending positions in front of the goal, attacking space is always more readily available on the wings (flanks) than in the middle of the field.

Good teams know this and adapt their attacking strategy accordingly. By playing or taking the ball wide they can get behind defenses; get the opposition turning towards their own goal; entice defenders out of the center creating an opportunity to capitalize on the situation — by playing in cross balls, for instance.

Space is available on wings.

Other principles of team play must be considered in effective team strategy — the need for PENETRATION and the WILLINGNESS TO TAKE RISKS are two.

Another is the principle of MOBILITY where confusion can be caused in the opposition defense by players' making runs and interchanging positions.

In defense, DISCIPLINE and PATIENCE will always be important . . . as will COMPACTION and BALANCE.

Allen Wade, the former Director of Coaching in England, in his book "The FA Guide to Coaching and Training" (see Bibliography) published 1968, wrote a detailed description of the Principles of Play. It is recommended reading. This was important documentation of the key team considerations, and has had a profound effect on coaching internationally.

Team Shape

Keeping in mind the principles of team play — in particular the requirements of all round ATTACKING SUPPORT and DEFENSIVE SUPPORT, UTILIZING THE WIDTH, and awareness of the advantage of exploiting and implementing the OFFSIDE rule, a TEAM SHAPE will be established irrespective of the numerical arrangement of players.

In the illustration the team shape is poor. Both teams have allowed themselves to become stretched

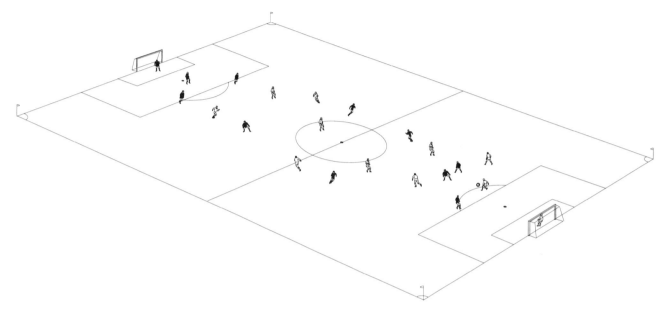

Elongated shape due to both teams being stretched end to end.

from end to end. Players are not in positions to support one another ; no advantage has been taken of the offside rule; and the elongated "shape" gives little opportunity for players to exploit the areas on the flanks. Only the "big boot" has any chance of success here and these tactics were abandoned by Coach Noah and his team, long ago!

With both teams taking full advantage of the protection that the offside rule offers, an almost diametrically-opposite shape can result — as shown in the second illustration.

English soccer in the '70s and '80s found this situation occurring in many games.

It makes for very tight, aggressive, often exciting play but with many whistles for offside. It is not recommended for young players still in the development phase. They would not have the experience to apply the tactics, nor would it greatly help the development of skill, other than defensive skills. From an attacking perspective, the supporting positions are too tight.

The "SHAPE" shown in the third illustration is a good one.

The team is supporting itself well from the back, through the midfield to the front players. The triangles between players are evident all over the field (see illustration on page 18). The ability to use the width of the field through the positioning of players is apparent.

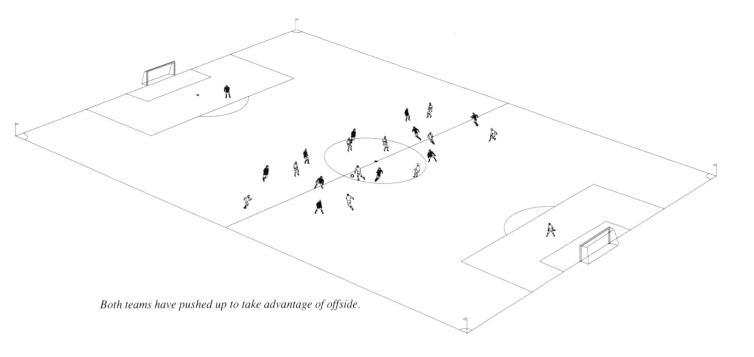

Both teams have pushed up to take advantage of offside.

The team in the illustration below is in the attacking mode and is spread out more than if the team was defending and therefore compacting to withstand an assault on its goal.

After successfully defending, and on regaining possession, a team should once more spread itself

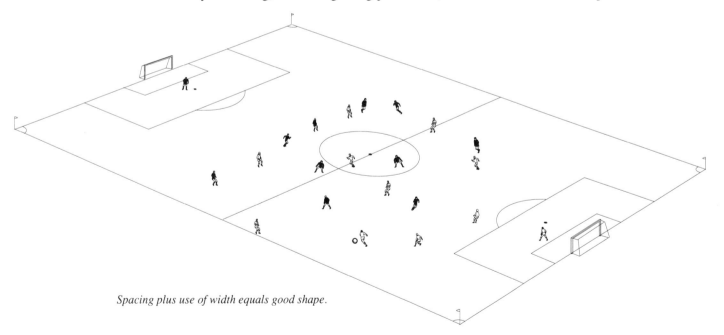

Spacing plus use of width equals good shape.

outwards, backwards and forwards, to give the space to play and the attacking shape. It's like breathing in and out. Expanding and contracting.

Naturally, as the ball moves, each player moves. But the basic team shape tends to be retained. However, from an attacking point of view, the team shape must only be the base from which players

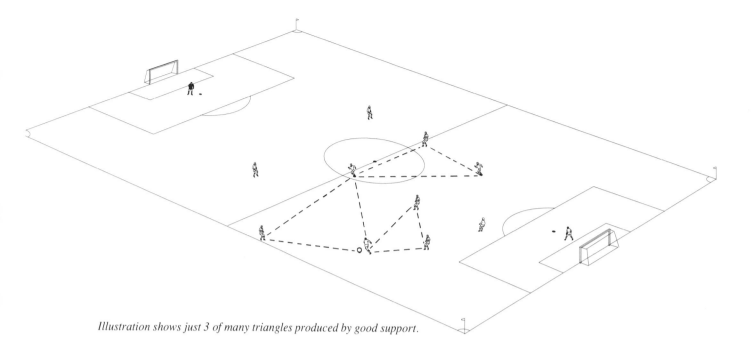

Illustration shows just 3 of many triangles produced by good support.

may spring forward. Every encouragement should be given for players to take calculated risks — particularly in the final "third" of the field.

When possession is lost, all players must react instantly and fall back into the defending team shape — to compact and consolidate.

Team shape, as I continue to point out, is not a numbers game — and the deployment of players in the illustrations shown is not meant to suggest a 4-2-4, 4-3-3 or any specific numerical arrangement.

X **POSITION OF BALL**

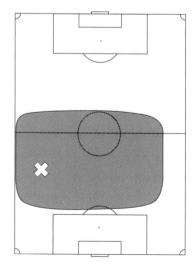

*Attacking shape
in build-up from back.*

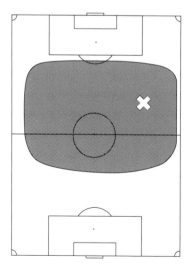

*Attacking shape
in attacking half.*

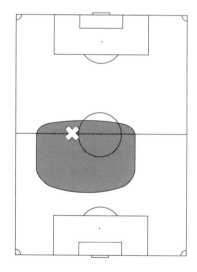

*Defensive shape showing
compaction goal-side of ball.*

Each coach in agreement with players should put together a system of play which will include basic field positions — THAT IS BEST FOR THOSE PLAYERS — and not employ a system successfully used by Argentina, Liverpool FC, or whomever.

What a team coach should borrow from the top teams of the world is their insistence in having good defensive and attacking support, and their solid understanding of the principles of attack and defense that produce a well-balanced "TEAM SHAPE."

Key Considerations in Team Shape

The "Team" unit should be considered like a giant amoeba, a single cell, moving up and down the field changing its position and to a lesser extent its shape to meet the demands — but always retaining its "ONENESS."

The "shape" of the team and its actual position within the field of play will be determined by:

   a) The position of the ball.

   b) The deployment of players by the opposition.

   c) The mode of play (whether attacking or defending).

Good "shape" requires:

   1. Good support – linking the back, the midfield and the front players.

   2. The right distances and angles between players – giving triangles throughout the team.

   3. A team understanding of how "offside" should be addressed collectively.

   4. Utilization of width – in the attacking mode; or consolidation and compaction – in the defensive mode.

The Soccer Jigsaw

Think of soccer coaching as a jigsaw puzzle. One problem with the soccer jigsaw is that the reference picture enabling us to piece the puzzle together is the game of soccer, and this picture is held within our mind's eye.

Without the advantage of a "real" picture to "see" and to compare, the coach not only has to be able to "see" the "big picture" but also to be able to assemble the practise "pieces" in that big picture. This has to be accomplished not only in the coach's mind, but in the minds of the players.

When we as coaches put on a practise, we are cutting our own piece of the puzzle from the game of soccer, working on that part, and then hoping the players will understand where that "piece" goes in the big picture. The greater number of pieces there are, the smaller they are, and the more difficult it is to put one little piece back in place.

In "team coaching," there is a strong case for cutting the "jigsaw" into as few pieces as possible — so that the players can see quite clearly just where that big piece fits.

Thirds of the Field

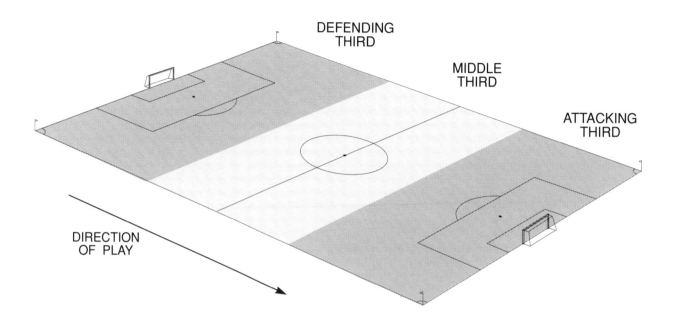

DEFENDING THIRD

MIDDLE THIRD

ATTACKING THIRD

DIRECTION OF PLAY

From a "strategy" perspective, it is helpful to think in terms of **thirds** of the field rather than **halves**. Certain things can occur in the Final or Attacking Third that would be irresponsible in the Back or Defending Third.

Attacking Third

The finishing zone of the field of play, where players should be encouraged (not criticized) when they take chances such as attempting to run and dribble past two or three defenders. Positive play here can pay big dividends and a mistake that causes loss of possession is not as critical as it would be at the other end.

Middle Third

The build-up zone. Ball possession is of paramount importance in this area. Great judgment is required in deciding whether to keep safe possession of the ball or play forward (penetration) to open up the defense — with the chance of setting up a scoring opportunity. Players frequently giving up possession in the Middle Third must be considered a poor risk in team terms.

Defending Third

The no-nonsense zone. Dribbling and back heel flicks by defenders may delight the crowd — and the opposing players — but not the rest of the team, nor the coach! "Safety first" has to be the maxim here — without resorting to panic play. Nevertheless, even though risks should not be taken, it is far better for the team if the ball can be brought out of the Defending Third in a controlled manner.

Moving the Ball Downfield

Other than long kicks from goalkeepers and rear defenders, there is a route available for building up attacks that increases the chances of success.

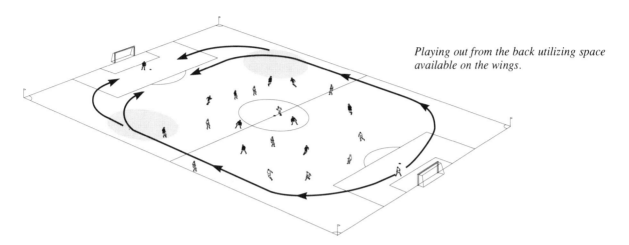

Playing out from the back utilizing space available on the wings.

With the ball at the back in controlled possession of the goalkeeper or the defenders, more often than not there is space to play out wide in the Defending Third.

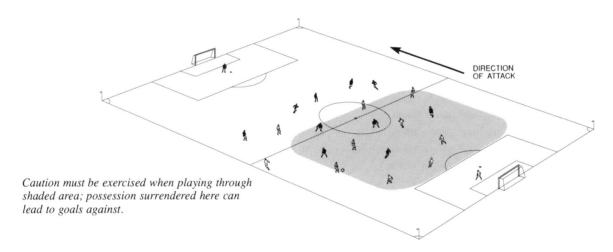

DIRECTION OF ATTACK

Caution must be exercised when playing through shaded area; possession surrendered here can lead to goals against.

Through the Middle Third, the safest build-up area is a 15-yard corridor from the touchline inwards — both sides of the field. That does not mean the central area of the field will not be used. But there are risks if possession is lost there, with less risk and less chance of a counter attack if the ball is lost on the flanks. If play becomes "closed down" by the opposition in the wide areas of both the Defending or Middle Thirds, a lofted ball played over the top into the wide spaces of the Attacking Third (see first illustration) is an effective — and safe — penetrating pass.

From wide positions — both in the Defending Third and the Middle Third — if build-up play is to take place on a consistent basis, there will be occasions when the ball will have to be played inside. Generally speaking, a good guideline is — WHEN THE BALL IS PLAYED INSIDE IT SHOULD BE FOLLOWED BY A BALL PLAYED "OUT." One "inside" pass followed by another "inside" pass — in the Defending and Middle Thirds — can often be intercepted or at least "disputed."

PRACTISE SECTION

The Game is the Teacher

In the previous books in the "Coaching" series ("Coaching 6, 7 & 8 Year Olds" and "Coaching 9, 10 & 11 Year Olds"), Bobby Howe and I continually stressed that "The Game is the Teacher." We recommended fun games and practises that we know work — where kids have fun and yet acquire the skills and understanding of the game through the circumstances they face in the practise. Kids "learn by doing" and also "learn by trial and error." Placed in the right learning environment, young players will acquire knowledge and skill — without being coached.

It would be nice if we could accelerate the learning by avoiding some of the trial-and-error process — by giving suggestions to the kids that would lead them straight to the correct way (trial and success). But let's face it, the best coaches in the world don't have ALL the answers!

One major aim of this manual is to provide practises that work; that challenge the players; that produce situations that will develop an understanding of team play while developing individual skills.

Presentation of the Practises

The Practise Section has been split into three parts.

Part I deals more with smaller units of the team — 3 and 4 players — in team games, where the "picture" is less complex than with larger numbers, e.g., 6, 7 and ultimately 11-a-side. The "bigger picture" is considered and applied in Parts II and III.

The practise suggestions in Parts I and III have been presented in a special way.

On each left-hand page is an illustration of the practise and an outline of the OBJECTIVES, the ORGANIZATION, the COACHING POINTS to look for and the CHALLENGE that should be presented to the players within the practise. This page will give you all the information you need to get the practise going — and working.

The right-hand page gives additional information, including the rationale behind the practise; the strengths and limitations of the practise; its suitability, applicability for different age groups; and where appropriate, some suggestions on how the practise can progress.

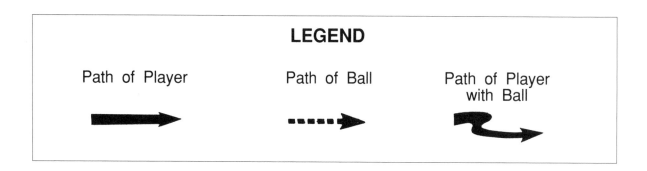

The Practises

Part I

Team Games

5 vs 2

Objectives

To develop supporting play; timing, pace and accuracy of passing; timing of runs.

Organization

- Groups of 10 whenever possible.

- Split into two teams of 5.

- 20 x 20 yards area.

- 5 vs 2 with other defenders waiting their turn.

- 5 attempt to keep possession from 2.

- Defending pair is changed on rotating basis every minute.

- Practise for 5 minutes in this situation, then defenders become the "attackers" and vice versa.

- Coach keeps supply of balls to help continuity.

Coaching Points

- Tell players "off the ball" to work continually at making good passing angles for players with ball.

- Encourage use of space available by spreading out.

- Require good passing techniques, pace of the pass and good "first touch."

- Make sure players "on the ball" are prepared to hold it and screen away from opponents if players "off the ball" are not available.

Challenge

- "Attacking five" scores a "goal" each time it completes 6 consecutive passes; the two defenders score a "goal" each time they win the ball and dribble it out of the area.

ADDITIONAL INFORMATION

Go to a practise of a top team of the world and there is a good chance you will see a 5 vs 2 practise taking place. It is a cornerstone of team practise.

A 5 vs 2 practise is used as the basis for developing good supporting play while at the same time giving each player plenty of ball contact, and therefore the opportunity of technique practise and of further developing the skills. It's a practise that requires good decision making and awareness by all players.

The 5 vs 2 also encourages composure on the ball. It is not always possible for the player to pass the ball. It could be that one's teammates have not taken up good positions or that one or both of the defenders have closed down the passing angles. This is the time to hold the ball, and to SCREEN the ball away from the opposition, while looking for support to become available to enable the passing sequence to continue.

Screening ball while waiting for support

STRENGTHS

- Excellent practise for developing team support.
- Assists development of effective defending in situations when defense is outnumbered.

LIMITATIONS

- 5 vs 2 situations don't occur too often in the modern game.
- Lack of direction of play and an authentic soccer objective (i.e., a goal) result in "possession" becoming an end in itself rather than a means to the end (i.e., creating a shot on goal).

PROGRESSIONS

- The coach should insist on nothing but the highest quality of performance. Going through the motions can produce bad habits. It is imperative to set objectives, make it competitive, so that players are motivated and challenged!
- The practise may be "progressed" by conditioning the game to two touches — even one touch. While this will eliminate the opportunity to hold and screen the ball, it will help improve touch and decision making. As well it will compel supporting players to work even harder to provide the passing angles.
- To increase/decrease the difficulty:

    The practise area size can be modified — larger makes it easier, smaller more testing.
    Numbers can be adjusted, e.g., 4 vs 2, 5 vs 3, 4 vs 1.

APPLICABILITY	
6, 7 & 8's	✘
9, 10 & 11's	✘
12-15's	✔
16 +	✔

The Numbers Game & Noah's Lark

Objectives

To develop good basic 1 vs 1 defending; to develop skilful 2 vs 2 defending (Noah's Lark).

Numbers Game

Organization

NUMBERS GAME

- Mark an area 30 x 20 yards.
- Goals approximately 5 yards apart.
- Divide teams evenly (e.g., 4 vs 4).
- Players on each team given a number, 1 – 4.
- Coach has supply of balls, calls a number (e.g., "three") rolls in a ball with the "threes" coming out to play 1 vs 1.
- Goals scored below knee height.
- Ball can be played back to "goalkeepers" who must play it back "one touch."
- Each pair competes for approximately 20 seconds. If ball goes out of play, coach can roll in another.
- "Goalkeepers" must defend collectively and must stay on goal line (otherwise penalty given — 6 yards from goal).
- No handling by "goalkeepers."
- With large numbers (e.g., 12 – 16) organize two practise fields (assistant coach).

NOAH'S LARK

- Organization as Numbers Game with pairs.
- Numbers given (12 players / 6 pairs easily occupied in one area).
- Other rules as Numbers Game.

Coaching Points

- Discourage defenders in 1 vs 1 from diving into challenge (and being easily beaten).
- Encourage defender to move in early and quickly to "close down" attackers and then to be patient, controlled and balanced.
- Encourage "hustling" defender to half turn and "channel" attacker away from shooting position.
- In Noah's Lark encourage good communication — who is to challenge the ball? Which way should the attacker with the ball be sent?

Challenge

- To outhustle and outscore the opposition.

Noah's Lark

ADDITIONAL INFORMATION

The Numbers Game is simply 1 vs 1. It is excellent for basic defending and exciting 1-on-1 attacking. The "team" benefit of this practise is the establishment of good defending habits and skills.

One man cannot be a team, but if basic 1 vs 1 defending is a weakness of some players on the team it will negate the benefits of any collective defensive system. Defensive supporting play must be arranged according to the position of the ball (as well as opponents). Much of the success of collective defensive play will depend on the ability of the player containing the opponent with the ball — the 1 vs 1 confrontation.

Also the **immediate defensive support** — i.e., the player covering the defender containing the opponent with the ball is the most critical (see the Noah's Lark practise). While the **secondary support**, i.e., the other defenders giving the defensive team shape, is obviously very important, it will only be effective if the "hustler" (the containing player) and the first (immediate) supporting player defend well.

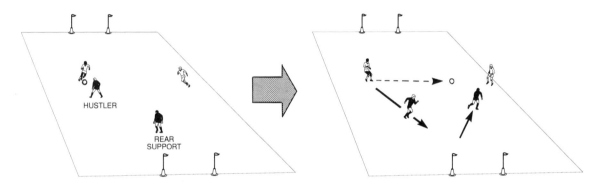

1 vs 1 defending with immediate rear support   *Pendulum change of defenders*

Notice in the second illustration that in the simple 2 vs 2 situation, when the ball is passed the "hustler" and first support change their roles "pendulum style." The "hustler" must not follow the pass.

STRENGTHS
- Poor defending in the Numbers Game and Noah's Lark will be obvious to all. Thus, there is an encouragement to learn FAST!
- It is a highly competitive, as well as an entertaining method of practise.

LIMITATIONS
- Good team defending is more complex than 1 vs 1 and 2 vs 2, requiring greater co-operation and positional considerations because of the larger numbers. Sooner or later, practise has to progress to larger numbers.

PROGRESSIONS
- Do not modify the practise. Progress to the larger numbers in practises such as the Zone Game (page 34), Attack vs Defense (page 60), and the Man Marking Game (page 56).

APPLICABILITY	
6, 7 & 8's	✔
9, 10 & 11's	✔
12-15's	✔
16 +	✔

Micro Soccer™

Objectives

A 3 vs 3 game with the basic tactical elements of the 11-a-side game, including goalkeepers, throw-ins, corners, with the principal aim of developing good attacking and defense support, "first touch" and accurate passing.

Organization

- Field size 25 x 35 yards (smaller for younger players).
- Six-yard "boxes" within which designated goalkeeper may handle — marked by cones or lines.
- Center line marked by cones / lines.
- Each player takes a turn in goal, for three minutes.
- When ball goes out of play, game is re-started by:
    Side line – throw-in (or pass-in)
    End line – goal kick or corner kick depending on which player last touched ball.
- After a goal re-start with either goal kick or center kick (if center — opponents must retreat to own six-yard line).
- In practise with numbers greater than six, either have two 3 vs 3, or if less than 12, have separate practise operating and rotate players in and out of the 3 vs 3 game.

Coaching Points

- Encourage the use of the width, particularly when rear player (sweeper/keeper) has the ball.
- Instruct keeper to come out and assist fellow attackers from behind.
- Define sweeper/keeper role as critical. Keep goalkeeper disciplined and calculating — not out of position on "wrong side" of ball.
- For good defending insist on a "hustling player," immediate supporting player, and secondary supporting player.
- Emphasize that ball possession is critical.
- Encourage "Keep Ball" play without allowing play to become overly negative.

Challenge

- To outscore the opposition.

ADDITIONAL INFORMATION

The game of soccer is played in triangles. In 11 vs 11, play should produce a series of triangles spaced out all over the field (see Support Play and Team Shape). Yet in a "phase of play" — for instance, when the ball is progressed after a throw-out by the goalkeeper from the back of the field to the front — there may be only 2 or 3 players involved in that phase. During that "phase of play," the rest of the team must take a secondary supporting role — positioning; ready for a final pass or a cross; or covering in case the ball is lost.

While employed as the Youth Coach at Liverpool, I introduced 3-a-side tournaments for the young professionals each Wednesday morning. Before long, the Head Coach (Manager) Bill Shankly asked me to organize the tournament to include all the pros — first team players included. I thought I had brought something new to the club. What I did not know then was Coach Shankly had introduced 3-a-side play when he first came to the club — to encourage players who played together in the same area of the field to gain a greater understanding of each other, in terms of their respective strengths and weaknesses.

Thus he selected the 3-a-side teams so that a right side defender played with a right midfielder and right winger; or two strikers with a central midfielder, and so on.

Three is the basic team unit of soccer — allowing the 3 elements always required in attacking play — *man with the ball, forward support* and *rear support.*

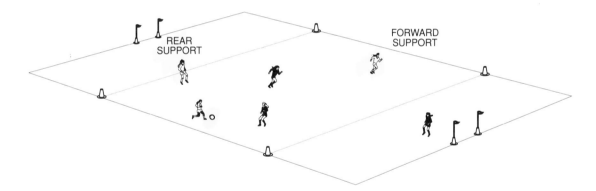

STRENGTHS
  * Gives many touches of the ball. Everyone is involved. Excellent developer of support play.

LIMITATIONS
  * Small field forces a "short passing game" without the opportunity to open up play or switch play with longer passes.

PROGRESSIONS
  * In our Micro Soccer game, *rear support* is provided by the *sweeper/keeper,* but the game can be modified to have no handling of the ball but with smaller goals. This encourages more inter-change of functions.

APPLICABILITY	
6, 7 & 8's	✔
9, 10 & 11's	✔
12-15's	✔
16 +	✔

4-a-side

Objectives

To develop team play on defense and attack in a demanding yet enjoyable game; to encourage *3rd Man Running*.

Organization

- Mark area 25 x 35 yards.

- Goal 4 yards apart.

- 6 yard marks for goalkeeping handling zone.

- 4 vs 4 — plus substitutes if desired.

- One player designated goalkeeper — allowed to handle in 6 yard area.

- Goalkeeper is changed frequently on rotating basis.

- Half-way mark — optional — for kick-offs; alternatively, game can restart after a goal with a goal kick if coach wishes.

- Throw-ins or kick-ins (at discretion of coach).

Coaching Points

- When the goalkeeper has the ball, keep one player pushing as far forward as possible.

- Keep other two players split wide to give diamond shape — as the starting base to build an attack.

- In "fluid play," make all players aware of the position of the others — in particular the "3rd man."

- Have defenders take up good basic defending positions, yet stay aware of the "3rd man" — not get caught on the "blindside."

- Point out that sweeper/keeper becomes the "quarterback" of team play.

- Make timing of the run, and timing of the pass, critical in any "3rd man" play.

Challenge

- To outscore the opposition.

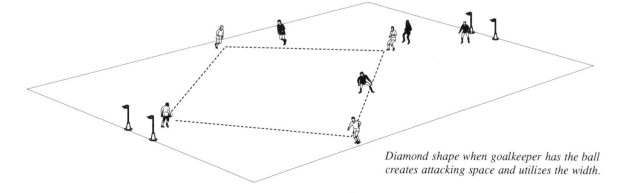

Diamond shape when goalkeeper has the ball creates attacking space and utilizes the width.

ADDITIONAL INFORMATION

Although 4-a-side is a natural extension of 3-a-side, it introduces many more possibilities — just by adding the extra player. Three players can only form one triangle at any one time. Four can make four triangles and the possibility of fast-changing permutations.

The 4-a-side game also provides frequent opportunities of exploiting the attacking play known as *3rd Man Running*, where two players combine to allow a 3rd player to make a run often undetected by the opposition. 3rd Man Running is one of the most skilful and difficult aspects of attacking play (see illustration).

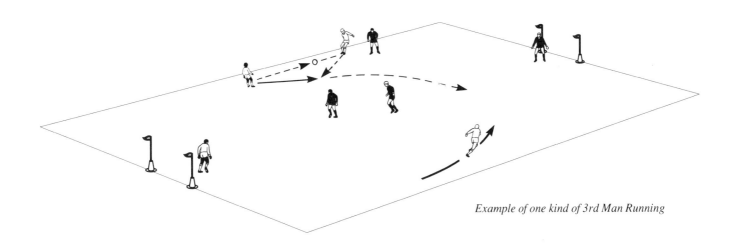

Example of one kind of 3rd Man Running

The small numbers still give ample opportunity of ball contact, while allowing the development of combination play on attack and on defense.

STRENGTHS
- Excellent game for developing team play while giving plenty of opportunities for "ball contact" for all players. Allows the development of 3rd Man Running situations.

LIMITATIONS
- Like Micro Soccer, 4-a-side is still confined to a relatively small area compared to the full 11-a-side field. Consequently, it reduces the opportunity of playing longer passes and the alternative of switching the play from one side to the other.

PROGRESSIONS
- Increase the numbers (e.g., 5 vs 5, Attack vs Defense).

APPLICABILITY	
6,7 & 8's	✘
9,10 & 11's	✔
12-15's	✔
16 +	✔

Zone Game

Objectives

To encourage skilful collective attacking — including "3rd man" and "blind side" running; to develop good collective defending.

Organization

- Mark area 30 x 25 yards — plus additional 5-yard "end zones."
- 3 vs 3 — plus substitutes if desired.
- "Goal" scored when attacking team dribbles or passes the ball into the end zone and is "touched down" with sole of foot.
- A "no-slide tackling rule" can be imposed to avoid unnecessary injuries.
- Coach keeps supply of balls to maintain continuity.
- Substitutes help recover balls that go out of play.

Coaching Points

- When two teammates are interpassing, advise 3rd attacker to look for penetrative run on the "blind side" of opponents.
- Encourage determined dribbling when teammates are "occupying" the covering defenders.
- Point out that cross-over runs by two attackers will confuse defensive organization.
- Have the three defenders organize themselves to:
  (a) contain player with ball, and
  (b) cover and mark the dangerous spaces and so avoid being drawn over from supporting positions by forward runs and cross-over runs.

Challenge

- To outmaneuver, and outscore the opposition.

ADDITIONAL INFORMATION

The 3 vs 3 Zone Game (shown opposite) is very demanding. It is extremely testing for the players — and the coach!

STRENGTHS

- Excellent game for encouraging quality attacking and near-perfect defending.

LIMITATIONS

- Will still need to be related to the "bigger picture" of the 11-a-side game — although many phases of defending rely on smaller units for their main success (e.g., Back Four).

PROGRESSIONS

Don't think it is necessary to advance the practise in terms of numbers. "Progress" can be made within the existing game.

However, at the right time there is a logical development of the practise when — and only when — the players are ready for it. In the 4 vs 4 Zone Game shown below, the organization is more complicated, the "refereeing" more difficult, and the "awareness" required by all players more acute.

The organization and rules of play in the 4 vs 4 Zone Game are identical to the 3 vs 3, except:

- A larger area is used (40 x 30 yards plus 5-yard end zones).
- In addition to the "goals" of the 3 vs 3 Zone Game, additional "goals" can be scored by an attacking player running into end zone "unmarked" — providing the team of that player has undisputed possession of the ball.
- Zone judges are placed on the side of each zone.
- One point is given for the "unmarked" run into the end zone. A "touchdown" goal equals four points.
- Attackers making forward run appeal to the zone judge for a point by raising arm.
- Judges raise arm if point is awarded.
- Play continues regardless.

PLEASE NOTE: "Unmarked" means that if the ball is played to the forward player in the end zone, the defender is caught out of position and unable to challenge immediately when the ball arrives (see illustration). In the example shown, "no point" is scored. The rearmost defender has recognized the wide run and adjusted slightly, so that he is still covering his fellow defenders, and yet in a position to move over and challenge if the ball was played to the wide attacker.

The 4 vs 4 game encourages forward and "blindside" running; and demands perfect defending.

It can also be stressful for the "referee" and zone judges!

APPLICABILITY	
6, 7 & 8's	✘
9, 10 & 11's	✔
12-15's	✔
16 +	✔

Chip 'n Dale*

Objectives

To encourage good collective attacking support and penetrative play; to develop collective defending.

Organization

- Area marked approximately 40 x 35 yards depending on numbers.

- Teams split into two — half on the field, half in opposite "goal zone."

- Depending on numbers can be 3 vs 3, or 4 vs 4 or 5 vs 5 — on the field.

- Goals are scored by chipping the ball into the hands of players inside the "goal zone."

- Goals only count if the ball does not touch the ground and the ball is caught within the goal zone.

Coaching Points

DEFENDERS

- Instruct one player to hustle player with the ball, not to "dive in" and so prevent the "chipped shot."

- Have immediate support player alert to movement of other players, while maintaining the "first support" position.

- Make secondary defensive support player(s) aware of forward and diagonal runs, and be prepared to "track down" without sacrificing defensive "shape."

ATTACKERS

- Tell players that accurate one and two-touch passing will break down defensive organization.

- Make player on the ball aware that fake and dribble can open up angle for chip.

- Point out that running "off the ball" and interchanging of positions will disrupt defensive organization.

- On-the-field players must react immediately when the ball is given up to the opposition — to prevent the quick counter-attack (and the first-touch chip shot).

Challenge

- To deny space to the opposition; to open up the defense of the opposition; to outscore the opposition.

ADDITIONAL INFORMATION

In collective defending, it is not sufficient merely to put cover on the player hustling the opponent with the ball. Other key considerations in defending are:

1. The distances supporting players should be from one another — and the opposition.
2. What adjustments in position need to take place as the ball is dribbled or passed — see defensive support and 2 vs 2 (page 13, 28 & 29).
3. Should a defender "track" a player who runs forwards (or sideways, or backwards) and risk losing the defensive "shape?"

This game will help the above considerations. The game in itself will be "the teacher."

The Game is the Teacher. The defensive support players must learn
how to adjust if a wide attacker makes a forward run behind the defense.

STRENGTHS

- Excellent learning situation for collective defending; develops good attacking skills and collective attacking team play.

LIMITATIONS

- The situations and the decision making are less complex than 11-a-side play.

PROGRESSIONS

- Introduce the alternative of playing the ball back to teammates off the field. Two players from each team go behind end line and are available for back passes if teams cannot play forward. End players have two-touches only (see illustration).

* Chip 'n Dale named after Dale Mitchell (NASL, MISL and Canadian National player) because of his uncanny ability to make space and chip accurately when performing in this practise.

APPLICABILITY	
6, 7 & 8's	✘
9, 10 & 11's	✔
12-15's	✔
16 +	✔

The Practises

Part II

Shadow Play

INTRODUCTION

Ronnie Moran, the Liverpool coach, with a twinkle in his eye, once said: "They spoiled the game of soccer when they introduced opposition. Until then it had been easy."

No doubt about it. Opponents have a nasty habit of upsetting the game plan.

Although opponents are a necessary fact of life in soccer, there is still a good case for practising patterns of team play WITHOUT OPPOSITION. The practise method is known as SHADOW PLAY.

Shadow Play is 11 vs 1. The "1" is the opposing goalkeeper. Patterns of play are developed on the field so that players begin to appreciate the types of passes to make; the positions to take up; the timing of runs to coincide with the passes (and cross balls) in order to produce a successful attack.

The absence of opposition allows the practise to flow and the patterns of play to become understood and established. Great care must be taken to avoid unrealistic plays which would break down in the presence of opponents. Bad habits established in practise will be punished later in 11 vs 11 play. The players — and in particular the coach — must use their imaginations to appreciate what will work in a true game circumstance, and what will not.

Let us first look at the illustrations to see how SHADOW PLAY is organized and how it operates.

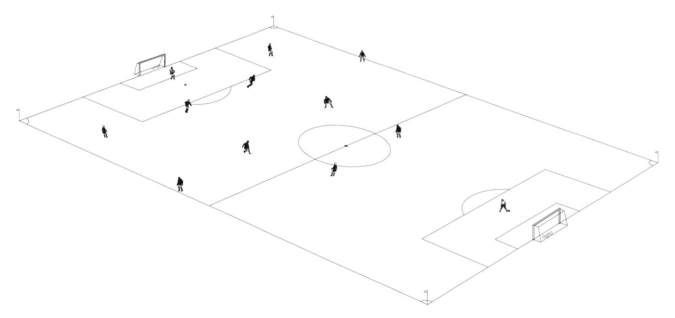

STARTING ORGANIZATION

- Two goalkeepers are in opposite goals with a supply of balls in each goal net.

- The goalkeeper of the 11-a-side team starts with a ball in his hand.

- The field players deploy themselves for a kick or throw from the goalkeeper.

- The coach can direct the goalkeeper to kick or to throw. For practise purposes it is better to throw more often than kick.

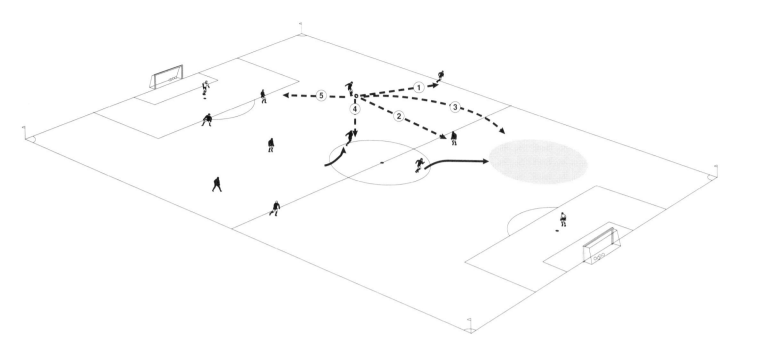

Play has begun with a throw from the goalkeeper to the left side defender.

The player with the ball, given with the deployment of players shown in this arrangement has several options:

Play the ball wide to the flank player — **1**

Play the ball forward into the feet of the first front striker — **2**

Play a lofted ball over the top of the opposition into the attacking space for the second striker making a run from a center field position — **3**

Play a pass inside to the supporting midfield player — who can then set up a pass to either the wide player or the front players — **4**

On the instruction of the coach, the ball can be played backwards or returned to the goalkeeper — as it might be in a game if the other options are closed off — for the back player or goalkeeper to start again, with a pass or throw to the opposite side — **5**

Play continues in a realistic way until a strike on goal ends with a goal, or the ball goes out of play — or the opposing goalkeeper secures the ball.

Sometimes the ball goes over the sideline through a misplaced pass. Play should be re-started with a throw-in.

This is the basic method of SHADOW PLAY. However, there are many developments which will add interest and life to this practise method. We will come to these shortly. Before that, let's look at how to introduce Shadow Play for the first time.

Introducing Shadow Play to the Team

- Don't set your expectations too high first time out.
- Describe Shadow Play as a *practical team talk*. Initially "walk through" the routine, talking about "team shape" and the positions players should take up as the ball is moved. It could be beneficial to show the concept of Shadow Play with the aid of a Tactical Chart or Chalk Board for 3 to 5 minutes before moving to the field.
- As they gain an understanding of the concept of Shadow Play — move from "walking through" to "jogging through" the sequences.
- Don't spend too long in the first session — 10 to 15 minutes will be ample.
- Consider using a mini-soccer field for the first session, i.e., across half a full field with two improvised goals, so that you can maintain easy contact with the players and they with one another. This way the concept can be more easily explained and understood.
- It will take a little while for the players to begin to understand the practise system.
- If everything does not go smoothly first time out, don't be discouraged. The dividends gained from Shadow Play in team play will be great — even though initially you may feel disappointed or you experience some "player resistance."
- Try limiting each player to two touches, maximum, each contact. This will cause players to support in realistic positions.

As the Shadow Play gains momentum, a few **DON'TS**:

1. **DON'T** allow too many square passes, nor too many ground cross-field passes through the midfield. Most times these will not work in the game.

2. **DON'T** let the play persist in the same direction if the players have indulged themselves in several tippy-tappy short passes. In the real game, too many passes in one area will draw in the opposition, and so the play should be "switched" to the opposite side — either by players passing back and across the back line to the other side; or by a direct cross-field pass over the top of the midfield area to the opposite flank.

3. **DON'T** forget that offside will apply in real game situations — so **DON'T** allow the strikers to run too far forward into unrealistic advanced positions.

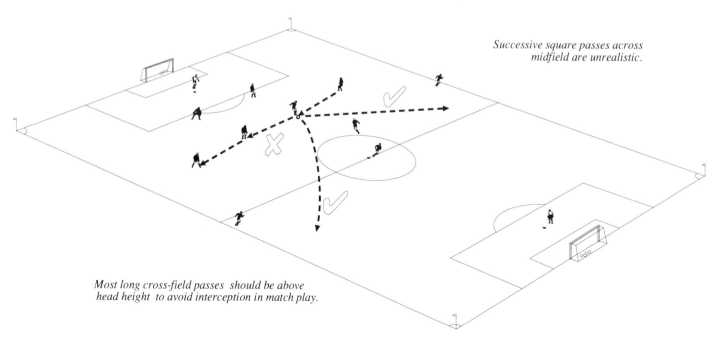

Successive square passes across midfield are unrealistic.

Most long cross-field passes should be above head height to avoid interception in match play.

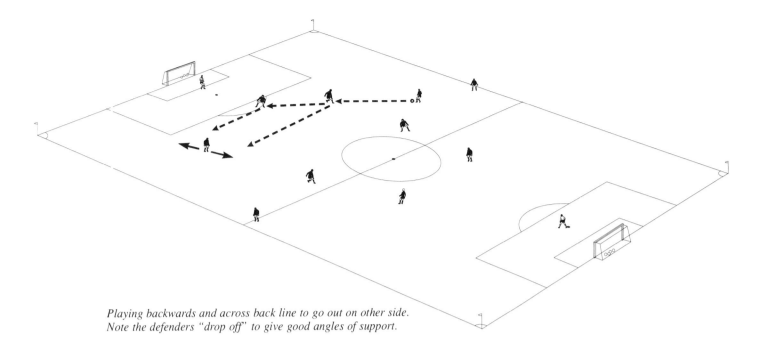

Playing backwards and across back line to go out on other side.
Note the defenders "drop off" to give good angles of support.

The coach, in implementing Shadow Play, will need to direct the play and "fire" the imagination of the players with "play-by-play" instructions. Later, the players will perform with a minimum of help from the coach — where the players themselves can show leadership and direct the flow of the practise and the changes of direction of play.

Shadow Play Methodology

After the completion of the first attack, the majority of players will be in the attacking half of the field. The goalkeeper will have either retrieved the ball out of his goal, or made a save, or have watched a shot go harmlessly by the goal.

Whatever, the goalkeeper starts the next phase with the ball in hand. With numbers of 12 as we have here (we will cover the larger player numbers later), there are three main methods of returning the ball to the other goalkeeper to start over again.

1. Ball is punted as far down the field as possible. This gives the goalkeeper kicking practise. The ball is then allowed to run through to the other goalkeeper or, if necessary, is helped back to the goalkeeper by the recovering defenders. While this takes place, the players fall back into the basic *team shape*, ready for the starting goalkeeper to begin another attack.

2. An alternative method is for the ball to be thrown by the goalkeeper to the coach, who dribbles the ball downfield with the rule that no one can tackle the coach. The team falls into its *defensive shape* relative to the ball. The coach can look at the covering positions while moving forward. And, as the coach dribbles the ball forward, instructions can be given to certain players to allow the coach to take the ball past them. These players are then on the "wrong side" of the ball, and are not required in this phase of practise to "recover" back into good defending positions, as they would in a game. The coach can then stop play to see how the defenders on the "goalside" have adjusted their positions and to see the *defensive shape*. Finally, the coach plays

the ball back to the goalkeeper or behind the defenders for them to recover the ball and begin their next attack downfield.

3. This method is the most interesting and entertaining one. After the initial attack, the ball is played out in the reverse direction in just the same way. Now the players find themselves operating in the very opposite positions to their customary roles.

Thus a striker becomes a defender; a right winger, a left full back; and so one. Only the central midfield players are spared a complete contrast. This is not only good fun — but good practise.

- Right-footed players are encouraged to use their left — and vice versa.

- Back players begin to understand how they can help front players — particularly with the quality of their passes.

- Front players begin to understand how important it is to "show" themselves to back players in order to help their accuracy and quality of passing — and in particular to be a "target."

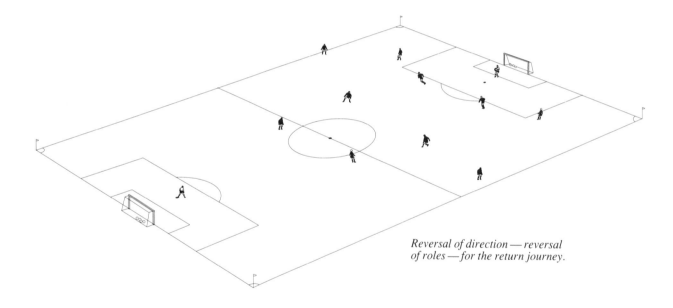

Reversal of direction — reversal of roles — for the return journey.

If the coach wishes, all three methods can be used at different times, as a way of returning to the original starting positions.

Shadow Play with Larger Numbers

More often than not, player numbers are greater than 12 — usually around 15 or 16, sometimes as many as 18.

Initially it may be necessary to work with just 12 to establish a clear understanding of the Shadow Play concept. That does not prevent the coach from "subbing" players in and out. There is also an advantage in starting on a "Mini" soccer field, so that the "walk-through" and "run-through" are accomplished with the players (and the coach) maintaining reasonably close contact.

Once the concept of Shadow Play has been established, it is a simple task to involve the extra players.

With 16 players go 11 vs 5

With 18 players go 11 vs 7

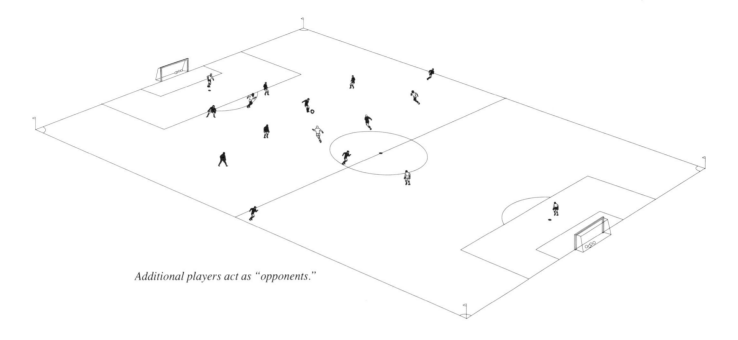

Additional players act as "opponents."

The inclusion of opposition will make it more difficult but, with numerical superiority, the team of 11 will still have less pressure and more space than in the 11 vs 11 game.

It is important that players are rotated in and out of the team of 11, so the 5 (or 7) "opponents" are not made to feel like second-class players.

With 5 or more opponents, the coach can work on additional parts of the team strategy during Shadow Play. For example:

1. A complete back line of opposing defenders.
2. Certain "opponents" could be assigned man-marking roles on midfield players, for example.
3. Attacking and defending corners / free kicks practised — with "opponents" taking up specific positions, even forming a "wall."

Shadow Play, with 16 – 18 players, is an excellent way of developing "re-start strategy" (kick-offs, corners, throw-ins, free kicks). It can be organized in a "natural" way so that 3 – 6 minutes of "set play" practise is followed by 5 minutes of fluid Shadow Play, and so on. The boredom of standing around for long periods at set play situations is therefore avoided.

Applicability of Shadow Play	
6, 7 & 8's	✗
9, 10 & 11's	✗
12-15's	✔
16 +	✔

Keep "Opposition" Interested

- With 5 – 7 "opponents," there is a further opportunity to change the system of returning the ball back to the normal starting position. This is achieved by allowing the small squad of "opponents" to interpass down the field finishing with a shot on the goal. While they are doing this, the 11-a-side team offers no opposition but jogs back into position ready for the next team attack.

- During an attack by the 11-a-side team, if the "opposition" players win the ball or intercept a misplaced pass their objective is to keep the ball for three consecutive passes as the 11-a-side team strives to regain possession. If they do, they score a goal (six passes give them two goals). Thus a game can be established with the "opposition" trying to outscore the authentic goals of the 11-a-side team.

Two-Team Shadow Play

With large numbers of players — many pro clubs will have as many as 22 — two teams can play "Shadow" at the same time, on the same field, but with two soccer balls.

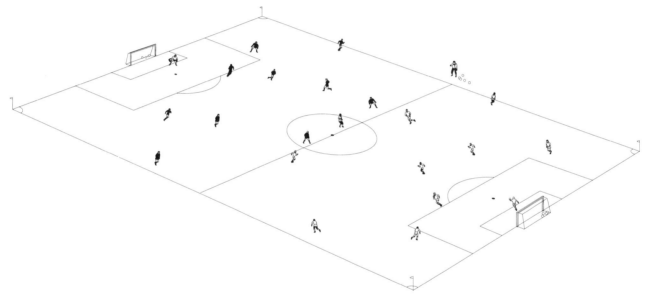

The coach must insist on synchronizing the start of each attack. Neither team can start an attack in the reverse direction before receiving a signal from the coach.

As with the "12-Man-Shadow," the teams can reverse their positions for the return attack. This method can work even with squads of 18, supplementing the squad by recruiting an assistant coach or two — even a fit and enthusiastic parent. Thus, two squads of 11 can be established. At the pro level I've sometimes pressed into service the trainer, the equipment manager — even myself! — to make up the two teams.

Further Options in Shadow Play

1. Condition the Shadow Play at times to "One Touch" per player. This game "condition" encourages good support, accurate passing, and develops the "first touch"; just as importantly, it forces the team to develop its "shape."
2. Use Shadow Play as part of the warm-up:

a) Begin with "walking" soccer — "Two Touches" maximum. No passes over 15 yards. Side-foot shots only. After two or three minutes, move into a slow jog (five minutes).

b) Two minutes stretching (players stay in field positions, coach shouts and demonstrates).

c) Increase to a faster jog and allow longer passes (25 yards) but no sprinting (five minutes).

d) Stretching — three minutes.

e) "All-Out" Shadow Play — sprinting, crossing, long passing, shooting, etc.

Total Time : 20 minutes.

3. With "Two-Team Shadow" it is simple to move into 11 vs 11 "Set Play" practise (corners / free kicks, etc.); or to put the patterns established in "Shadow" into normal 11 vs 11 play. Just take out one ball!

4. Use "Walk-Through Shadow" as a practical team talk — to give the players a better idea of the team plan.

5. Don't use "Shadow Play" for too long — maximum 20 – 25 minutes; normally 10 – 15 minutes.

*   Shadow Play can be modified in different ways to the ones shown here.

Summary

Without some form of Shadow Play, it is extremely difficult for a team to get a realistic appreciation of team play — the combination plays; the different "runs"; the quality of the passes and crosses; and the distances involved in supporting and passing. In the heat of the game, and with the spoiling tactics of the opposition, the strategy you are seeking to implement has less of an opportunity of being "patterned." Time and experience — trial and error over an extended period of time — may help establish a team pattern. But how many coaches (and players) can wait 10 years?

Postscript to Shadow Play

A few years ago, a rumor circulated the Merseyside area of England. Dave Russell, Coach of little Tranmere Rovers, the 3rd Division Club of the City of Birkenhead, on the opposite bank of the River Mersey from Liverpool, was agonizing his way through a long losing streak. Not an unusual situation for Tranmere! So Dave called his old friend, Bill Shankly — the coach of mighty Liverpool Football Club.

"Bill, I need some way of getting the team out of this slump."
"Why not try Shadow Play?" said Shankly.
"Tried it last week, Bill! And we still got beat!"
"Have you tried placing eleven garbage cans in different positions on the field to simulate opponents. Then the players have to dribble around them, pass to the side, or play balls over them."
"Great idea," said Dave. "We'll try it this afternoon."

Three hours later, 'Shanks' got another call from Dave Russell.

"What do I do now, Bill? The garbage cans just beat us 1 – 0!"

The Practises

Part III

Larger Numbers

Crossroads

Objectives

To develop team patterns when attacking crosses; development of crossing, shooting and heading skills; and timing of runs to attack crosses.

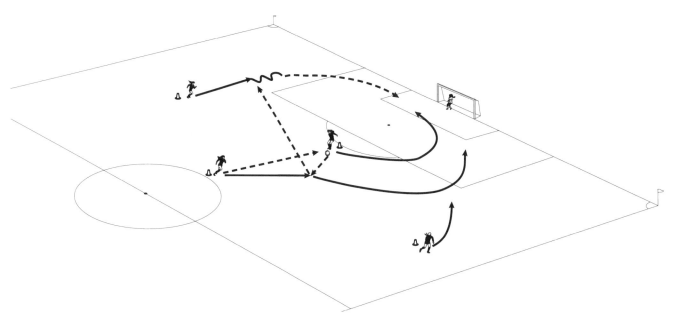

Organization

- Four stations are set up as in illustration.
- Goalkeeper(s) selected.
- Players evenly divided between stations, and attack in waves of four — one from each station (not shown in illustration).
- Play is started at the center circle and played to central front player.
- Ball is played by front player back to the starting player, who passes the ball to one of the two wide players.
- Front player and server move away from the crossing player and towards the penalty area to prepare to meet the cross to the near and far posts.
- Communication is essential in order for players to decide who goes "near post," and who goes "far post."
- Flank player not receiving ball supports the attack — but may if situation allows, take initiative to make one of the runs — even near post.

- "One Touch" only rule when receiving ball in penalty area.

Coaching Points

- Insist on good quality passing at start of the exercise.
- If "near-post" runner arrives too early, tell player to "spin" away and let next player move into "near post" space with third player making the "far post" run.
- Recommend deflection shots and "headers" at near post.
- Suggest heading down and away from keeper at far post.
- Have crossing player attempt to hit around the outside of the ball to bend cross away from goal and the goalkeeper.

Challenge

- For attackers, to perfect the patterns of attack — and to score; for goalkeeper(s), to keep goals to minimum.

ADDITIONAL INFORMATION

This is a very demanding, challenging and enjoyable practise — without the necessity of opposition.

There are three KEY parts to the practise:
1. The three passes that start the practise — the ball in, the set-up ball, and cross-field pass. In all cases the quality must be first class.
2. Quality of the cross.
3. Timing of the runs to the near and far post.

Key Considerations:
- The crossing player should aim for the spaces, not the player.

- The "cross" should be played into the near post space — head height or below, and slightly bending away from the goal.

- The slightly overheight / over-paced, near-post cross will end up the ideal far-post cross (giving the best of both worlds).

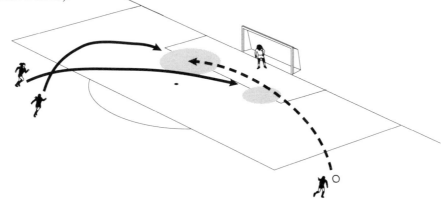

Ideal angles of runs, and target areas for cross.

The timing of runs is critical:
1. Near-post run has to be made early and fast — if time allows, should be a "bent run" to allow attacker to get on the "blindside" of the defenders, and in line with the cross.
2. Far-post run is less demanding as it would be wrong to be in too early "waiting" for cross. Coming in late allows the player to attack the cross and with momentum to add to the leap — if required.

STRENGTHS
- Even without opposition this is a challenging and realistic practise.

LIMITATIONS
- Inevitably there is much more pressure in the game — from opponents. However, as with Shadow Play, the "patterning," timing and execution must be acquired first.

PROGRESSIONS
- Add a defender to assist the goalkeeper — but only when the practise is succeeding without opposition.

APPLICABILITY	
6, 7 & 8's	✗
9, 10 & 11's	✗
12-15's	✔
16 +	✔

Big Shot

Objectives

To develop ability to create shooting angles and positions; to improve shooting from central areas.

Organization

- Mark area 30 x 25 yards, with half-way line.
- Two full-sized goals (portable or improvised goals with cones / poles).
- Two goalkeepers.
- 4 vs 1 (plus goalkeepers) in each half.
- A goalkeeper starts by rolling ball to one of four players.
- Four keep possession from the opponent while working to create a shooting position.
- Shots can only be taken from within own half.
- After shot the one advanced team player (the "sniffer") looks for scoring opportunities from rebounds off the goalkeeper, defenders or goal posts.
- Four players in possession may play back to their goalkeeper (or coach may decide to rule out this privilege).

Coaching Points

- Encourage players to try a strike for goal.
- Tell "sniffer" to always gamble on the possibility of a rebound.
- Have defending players take up good positions to block shots (even though confined to their half).
- Encourage goalkeeper to work at maintaining a view of the ball at all times.
- Teach goalkeeper to make good decisions relative to the situation, e.g., whether to catch or deflect the ball into non-dangerous areas.
- Encourage supporting play to give alternatives for shot or pass.

Challenge

- To outscore the opposition.

ADDITIONAL INFORMATION

Even though at the top level of soccer, many of the most effective attacks on goal are developed from the wide areas of the field, there is still a significant percentage of goals scored by working the ball through the central area of the attacking 'third' of the field. Long-range (20 yards or more) shooting, "one-two" sequences in and around the penalty area and rebound goals are all aspects of team attacking play that should be practised.

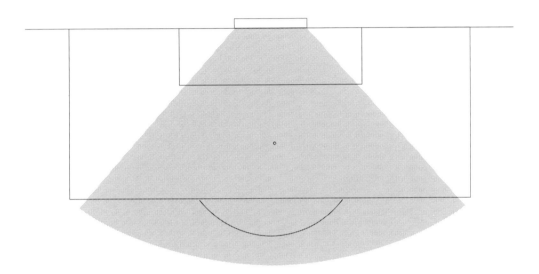

It is a fact that over 90% of all goals scored come from shots from within the area indicated in the illustration. Consequently, shooting practise must take place in this part of the playing field.

The "Big Shot" practise shown here is used in this and similar forms throughout the soccer world. It is highly recommended as a competitive and enjoyable way of developing the shooting skills.

STRENGTHS
- A realistic game situation giving repeated opportunities of shooting for goal.

LIMITATIONS
- Only covers one aspect of shooting for goal — from central attacks — albeit an important one.

PROGRESSIONS
- Goalkeeper can have the option of throwing the ball directly to front player (the "sniffer"). If that happens, one of the back players can be released to join the "sniffer" in the front half.
- Alternatively, a back player can play into front player ("sniffer") and follow the pass to join the "sniffer" in the front half for a one-two attempt at goal.

APPLICABILITY	
6, 7 & 8's	✗
9, 10 & 11's	✗
12-15's	✔
16 +	✔

4-Goal Game

Objectives

An all-action game encouraging collective attacking and "total defending"; in addition, the game highlights supporting play, good passing, ball control (the first touch in particular) and ball possession skills.

Organization

- Mark out square approximately 40 x 40 yards.
- Divide players evenly (6 vs 6, or 7 vs 7).
- Place 4 small goals (1 yard wide) five yards in from from each corner (use cones/poles).
- Score in any of four goals from the front only.
- Ball can be dribbled or played through and possession retained.
- Also 4 (or more) consecutive passes count as a "goal."
- Any interception, or deflection by opposition, breaks the sequence of passes.
- Goals through cones can be scored at any time in a passing sequence and multiple goals (passes or "cone" goals) scored in any possession.
- When ball goes out of play, re-start with "kick-in" (or throw-in if coach prefers).
- Phase in the rules when first introducing game (see opposite page).

Coaching Points

OFFENSE

- Emphasize that maintaining possession gives best chance of success.
- Advise players to be prepared to hold ball ("screening") if passing options are poor.
- Encourage switching play — particularly if one goal becomes "marked."

DEFENSE

- Emphasize importance of positional play to prevent easy scoring in any of 4 goals.
- Encourage everyone to work hard — otherwise opponents will easily maintain possession.
- Insist that opponent with the ball be "hustled."

Challenge

- Play in "sets" like tennis. First team to score six "goals" wins set. Play a best-of-three (or five) series.

ADDITIONAL INFORMATION

The 4-goal game is a good test for players — and an even bigger one for the coach.

The first task of the coach is to ensure the practise — its rules and objectives — are introduced and fully understood.

The following is the recommended method:

1. Explain the basic rules (see "organization" on the opposite page) but **at first do not introduce the "4 passes equals one goal"** rule. To start with just let them play.

2. Sooner or later, the players will realize they can easily stop the opposition by having 4 players mark the front of each goal. That is the time to introduce the 4-pass rule.

The toughest task for the coach is to keep count of the consecutive passes — by counting out loud — while keeping the "goal" score. If it is too testing, reduce each "set" to "3 goals to win" — that will relieve some of the scoring complexity for the coach! This is a very demanding activity for the players, so give them ample recovery time between each "set."

STRENGTHS
*   Excellent practise for developing the "first touch"; composure "on the ball"; and good team support. Also it forces players "to get their heads up" to assess the possibilities of passing or dribbling.
*   Excellent supplementary activity for "fitness" because of its all-action nature.
*   Promotes good collective team defending — any "defending" players opting out will increase the work load of others.

LIMITATIONS
*   Being able to score in any of 4 goals cannot properly simulate the conditions of 11-a-side play.

PROGRESSIONS
*   For younger players, reduce size of field and number of players, e.g., play 3 vs 3, or 4 vs 4. With older players, as they become more accomplished keep field size and team numbers large but increase number of consecutive passes to score (e.g., 5 or 6 etc.)

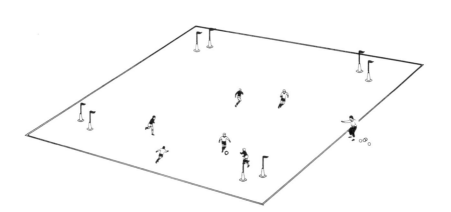

APPLICABILITY	
6, 7 & 8's	✗
9, 10 & 11's	✔
12-15's	✔
16 +	✔

The Man Marking Game

Objective

To establish both the individual and team discipline required for successful defending; to establish good 1 vs 1 defending habits; to practise reading the game (Sweeper Role); to encourage attackers to "elude" tight marking.

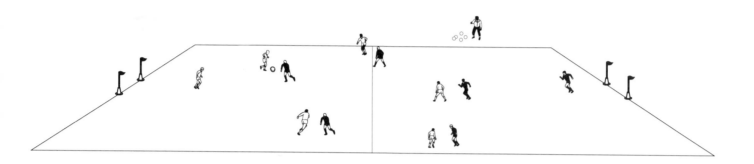

Organization

- Field sized according to numbers and ages (approximately 65 x 45 yards) with halfway line.

- Goals/poles are set up (4 yards wide).

- Squad is split up evenly (e.g., 6 vs 6).

- Every player is assigned a "Partner Opponent" from opposing team.

- One "pair" split to become the sweepers — "sweepers" are changed every five minutes.

- Each player can only mark and challenge his assigned opponent.

- The sweeper can challenge anyone.

- No one can challenge the sweeper.

- "Sweepers" are restricted to their own half of the field, and are limited to "two touches" maximum on each ball contact.

- Interceptions (not challenges/tackles) are permitted by anyone.

- No one is allowed to handle the ball.

Coaching Points

- Show players how to challenge opponent without "diving in" and being left trailing.

- Make each player aware of "opponent" at all times.

- When the attack breaks down have former "attacker" react immediately by attempting to recover to defending position "goal-side" of opponent.

- Carefully select the "match-ups" — two "lazy" players may come to an "agreement."

- Encourage players to get forward to score.

- Encourage player caught "wrong side" to get back if a teammate loses the ball — but don't criticize them if they are caught out when trying to make a positive forward run.

- Position "sweeper" to block an attack or to be available for a back pass from own team.

Challenge

- To outsmart your individual marking opponent both in attack and defense; and, as a team, to outscore the opposition.

ADDITIONAL INFORMATION

Through the years, the game of soccer has been caught in a controversy regarding which is the best system of defending — a "Man Marking System" with a spare player (sweeper) at the back, or a "Zone Defense" where players make themselves responsible for marking an area of the field and "mark" players who enter their "space."

Other sports such as football and basketball have faced the same dilemma. In truth, all systems of defending are a combination of the two — strict man-to-man marking does not work (what happens if one player is beaten?), and marking a "zone" leads to complications if the attacking team overloads one area by placing several players in the one space.

In today's soccer, more of the top teams of the world have a defensive system which is predominantly based on a "zonal" organization. But there are still many highly successful teams using a "man marking" strategy as their defensive base. The "Zone Game" described earlier in this segment requires "zonal" defending. Both the "Zone Game" and this practise will help develop good collective defending.

STRENGTHS

- No-nonsense yet demanding activity.
- Competitive and realistic in terms of 1 vs 1 defending and the requirement to "back track" to get "goal side" when possession is lost.
- Excellent practise to introduce the "sweeper" role.
- Good "attacking" practise in how to lose your "man."

APPLICABILITY	
6, 7 & 8's	✗
9, 10 & 11's	✗
12-15's	✔
16 +	✔

LIMITATIONS

- The "one man only" marking requirement excludes other important aspects of 11 vs 11 defending.
- Sweeper has "luxury" of not being challenged.

PROGRESSIONS

- Move from the "Man Marking" game into an Attack vs Defense practise, or into 11 vs 11 play, taking off the "man marking" condition of only being able to challenge one player. That brings the "marking" requirements into a more realistic circumstance.
- Remove "marking" condition and play a "free" 6 vs 6 or 7 vs 7 game, concentrating on good defense.

5-a-side

Objectives

To encourage good supporting play and use of the width of the field.

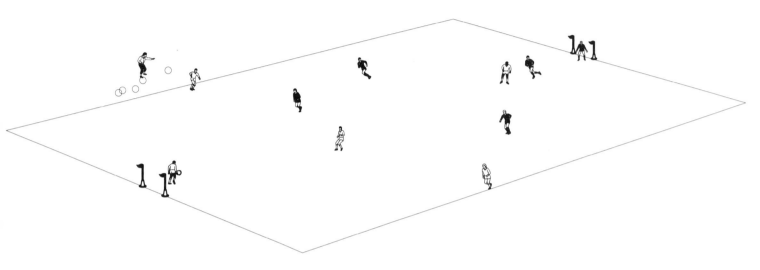

Organization

- Mark an area approximately 35 x 55 yards (¼ of full-sized soccer field).

- Improvise goals (or full-sized portable goals — if available).

- If improvised goals, specify height under which goals are scored — coach is the judge of what is or is not a goal.

- Designate goalkeepers and specify where they can handle the ball.

- If goalkeepers are not "regular" goalkeepers, change every five minutes.

- No offside — otherwise normal rules.

Coaching Points

- When goalkeeper has the ball, encourage players to spread and use width (see opposite page).

- If necessary, stop the game and show the possibilities that are being ignored.

- After losing ball, ask nearest defender to opponent with the ball to be patient and hustle opponent to "buy" time until teammates recover.

- Use "conditions" for short periods (e.g., two touch or one touch) to assist theme of session.

Challenge

- To outscore the opposition.

ADDITIONAL INFORMATION

For youth players between the ages of 12 to 15, the 5 vs 5 game is one of the best ways to encourage the key elements of team play in a situation understandable to players. In particular, supporting play, possession play and responsible collective defending can be developed. The 5 vs 5 game is a progression from the Micro Soccer (3-a-side) and the 4-a-side play recommended earlier.

In our previous coaching manuals, our recommendation was that Micro Soccer be the base development game for 6, 7 and 8 year olds, and 4-a-side the base development game for 9, 10 and 11 year olds.

The strong recommendation is that 5 vs 5 play be the base development game for 12 to 15 year olds — with a progression to 6-a-side and 7-a-side after that. It is interesting to note that professional players and their coaches favor the 7 vs 7 game as their base game.

If the 5 vs 5 game is used as a learning situation, the coach must ensure the game does not become merely a fun game. There is no reason at all why a 5 vs 5 (or a 6 vs 6, or a 7 vs 7) should not be played as a fun finale to the session. But if "team development" is the aim, there needs to be an insistence on a conscious effort being made to produce patterns of team play.

For instance, when a goalkeeper gains possession of the ball:

1. At least two players should break wide.
2. A forward player should push back onto the opposition — to become a target man with space in front to receive the ball.
3. One player should hold a central withdrawn midfield position — as insurance.

That initial structure (see illustration on opposite page) will give the space from which the goalkeeper can throw (or kick) the ball to begin the build-up of an attack.

Conditioning the game to "two touches maximum" per contact will force players to produce supporting play.

STRENGTHS
- A competitive situation providing realistic game conditions and good motivation for the players.

LIMITATIONS
- No offside rule (the practise would not function with it) tends to give less than realistic defending situations, and does not provide normal "penalty box" goalkeeping.

PROGRESSIONS
- Increase the numbers to 6 vs 6, or 7 vs 7, but make sure to increase size of field proportionately.
- 7 vs 7 gives additional possibilities with the use of width, plus the option of two advanced players working together. The increased numbers also allow more positive near and far-post runs (see "Crossroads").

APPLICABILITY	
6, 7 & 8's	✗
9, 10 & 11's	✔
12-15's	✔
16 +	✔

Attack vs Defense

Objectives

To develop attacking and defensive understanding and team strategy.

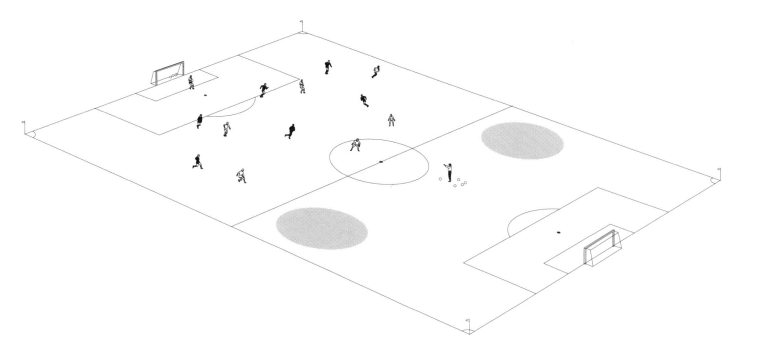

Organization

- Players are arranged in their team positions — in this example, 6 vs 6 plus a goalkeeper.

- The players start in one half of the field.

- Target zones are marked on either side of the field for the defending team to play out to and "score."

- Coach serves ball into attacking half.

- Normal attack takes place — if defenders (and goalkeeper) win ball, they attempt to play out.

- Defenders score by chipping the ball on one bounce into either target zone — or by dribbling or passing into a zone.

Coaching Points

- Outline briefly — preferably by walk-through demonstration — the expectations of the practise.

- If practise is not succeeding and you're sure of analysis, stop the practise and show what could have been done.

- Similarly, stop and show what was done well.

- Don't stop practise too much or interest will diminish.

- Discourage defenders from playing too many short passes.

- If defenders win the ball and then give it back foolishly, encourage attackers to punish the mistake.

Challenge

- Defense to outscore attack by getting more "zone goals" than "real" goals; and vice-versa.

ADDITIONAL INFORMATION

There is a variety of "Attack vs Defense" practises (sometimes called Phase of Play practise).

The practise suggestions on the opposite page can be readily modified to the particular needs of a team.

1. If the attacking patterns need developing and encouraging, the "attacking" group can be overloaded, e.g., six attackers versus four defenders, and so give a better opportunity for success because of less defensive pressure — see Shadow Play.

2. If the back defenders needed special attention then a four attackers vs six defenders practise could be organized (or three attackers vs six defenders). This would give the defense spare players.

3. A five attackers vs four defenders would force a "zone defensive system" as four cannot man-mark five.

4. Putting into a practise two or three midfield players and a back defensive line against a forward line and opposing midfield players would quickly result in something like an 8 vs 8, plus a goalkeeper, and therefore require a correspondingly larger practise area.

It is important to give the defenders a target other than just the success of the "spoiling" an attack. In the example opposite, we have used target zones in wide positions in the other half of the field. Small goals or target men (perhaps the coach and assistant coach) can be just as effective.

Remember not to be overly ambitious with your practise theme. Concentrate on one main topic, and one group of players (attackers or defenders). Total team strategy cannot be covered in one practise session.

STRENGTHS
- A realistic practise, simulating conditions closely resembling the full game, yet allowing the opportunity of concentrating on one main theme.

LIMITATIONS
- Unless carefully structured, players can find themselves running into unrealistic areas of the field, e.g., a left winger may wander across to the right flank. That would be alright if it was part of the game plan — but disruptive if not. Specify to players the positions they would be expected to take up.

PROGRESSIONS
- Increase numbers — eventually considering 11 vs 11 play.

APPLICABILITY	
6, 7 & 8's	✘
9, 10 & 11's	✘
12-15's	✔
16 +	✔

Mixed Bag

Objectives

To place field players and goalkeepers in decision-making situations with attacks developed from the flanks.

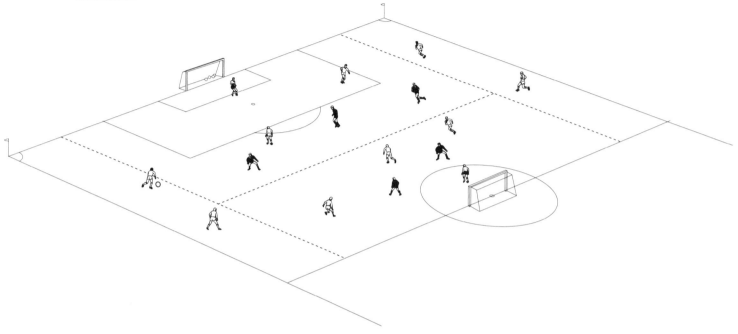

Organization

- Use half of a full-sized field. Mark out a 6-yard channel each side of field.
- Mark in a center line.
- The 2 players in each "flank channel" have no allegiance - they play for both teams.
- 3 vs 2 - plus a goalkeeper - in each half.
- When goalkeeper has the ball, the practise is always re-started by goalkeeper throwing to flank players.
- Flank players can pass to one another, overlap, cross the ball, or pass the ball in to the 3 attackers.
- Change the players' positions periodically to give everyone experience in different roles (except goalkeepers).
- Offside rule should be applied by coach.

Coaching Points

- Goalkeepers must work on good quality throws to wide players, and be encouraged to "switch" play.
- Goalkeepers must communicate their requirements; organize the defense; and adjust to changing situations.
- Quality of cross from wing players critical for successful attacking play.
- Three attackers in each half need to communicate and work "off" one another, with particular attention to "near-post" and "far-post" runs.
- The two defenders in each half have to work skilfully because they are outnumbered.

Challenge

- For the "wingers" - to deliver quality crosses; for the rest - to outmaneuver the opposition.

ADDITIONAL INFORMATION

While the practise will be more realistic using a portable regulation goal on the center line, it is not essential. If a portable goal isn't available, use corner flags to make the goal.

It is important that the 2 "wingers" on each side work in a realistic manner. For instance:

1. They should drop back to receive the throw from the goalkeeper; and space themselves like a wide defender and a winger would.

2. They should time their passes and runs, and make realistic overlap runs to set up for crossing the ball.

3. They should not move into the final part of their attacking corridor too early because that will take away their "crossing" space.

4. Ideally, the final set-up pass should be into space for the "winger" moving forward to cross first-time.

It is important for the coach to apply the offside rule, and to encourage goalkeepers and their defenders to keep the attackers as far out of the goal area as possible.

STRENGTHS

- Realistic, fast action, and highly-challenging practise. Thirty minutes or more can be spent without any risk of boredom. Everyone benefits. Excellent practise for goalkeepers.

LIMITATIONS

- The conditions of play limit other aspects of attacking play; defenders can only mark in a "zone" organization because they are outnumbered.

PROGRESSIONS

- Release one of the "wingers" to follow in a pass or cross.
- Release a defender to cross the center line to support the attackers (i.e., 4 vs 2).
- Release an attacker to run back into defending half to help outnumbered defenders.

APPLICABILITY	
6, 7 & 8's	✗
9, 10 & 11's	✗
12-15's	✔
16 +	✔

Super 8's

Objectives

To produce a fast-changing game with most of the critical decision-making ingredients of 11-a-side play, including off-side.

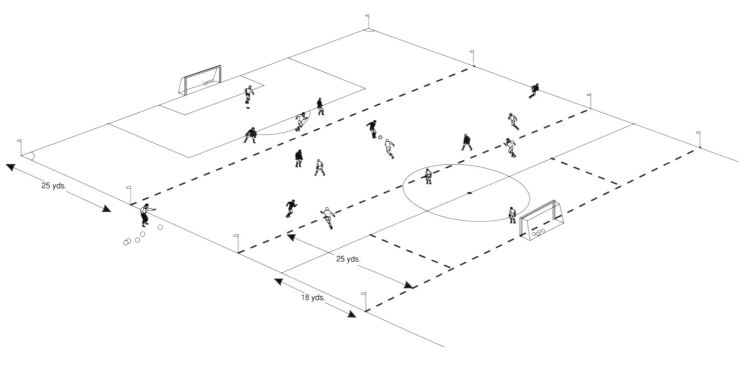

25 yds.

25 yds.

18 yds.

Organization

- Set up a line and regulation-sized goal 18 yards beyond center line.

- Mark in two 25-yard lines with coaching disks - if available use corner flags to emphasize 25-yard lines.

- If available use two people - assistant coaches, parents - to act as linesmen, stationed on opposite sides of field to coach at the 25 yard-lines (with flag or handkerchief).

- Normal rules of soccer, except that each team can only be offside beyond attacking 25-yard line.

- Consider narrowing field by 5 to 10 yards on each side if maximum regulation width (i.e., 74 yards).

Coaching Points

- Encourage goalkeepers and rear defenders to "utilize" offside to keep opponents away from goal.

- Encourage "total soccer", with players moving up and down field with no set positions; therefore playing "both ways."

- Encourage awareness, attacking support, width and defensive cover.

- Encourage goalkeepers to help "organize" the team.

Challenge

- To outscore the opposition.

ADDITIONAL INFORMATION

Most teams have a roster of 14 to 18 players. While 11 vs 11 play can be advantageous in developing team understanding, most teams cannot organize "in-house" 11 vs 11 play... but can play 7 vs 7 or 8 vs 8.

8 vs 8 - the "Super" game - is the best arrangement. This produces most of the questions and answers required of 11-a-side play - particularly when the team "plans" and team "positions" are not working, and players are forced to think for themselves.

However, "Super 7's" and "Super 9's" are quite acceptable.

The demanding nature of the Super 8's game will help develop the "two-way" player that is so desirable in modern-day soccer.

STRENGTHS

- Excellent 2-way soccer makes repeated demands on the skills and decision-making abilities of each player. First-class all-round development situation for goalkeepers.

LIMITATIONS

- There are few limitations to this practise, except that Super 8's lacks some of the ingredients of 11 vs 11 play because of the lesser numbers.

PROGRESSION

- The progression lies within the practise itself - through the further development of the players' individual and team abilities.

APPLICABILITY	
6, 7 & 8's	✘
9, 10 & 11's	✘
12-15's	✔
16 +	✔

"Full Field" Team Games

Several valuable "team" games can be played on a full soccer field even if numbers are not quite 11 vs 11. Here are two of them.

EVERYONE IN ATTACKING HALF

Teams from 9-a-side to 11-a-side. No goalkeepers. Goals only count if all players of attacking team are in attacking half of the field when goal is scored. If the defending team still has a player(s) in the other half of field when goal is scored, the goal counts double.

Objective: To encourage supporting play of whole team — from back to front; encourage the tactic of the team moving out as a unit after a clearance (using the assistance of the offside rule in match play).

APPLICABILITY	
6, 7 & 8's	✗
9, 10 & 11's	✗
12-15's	✔
16 +	✔

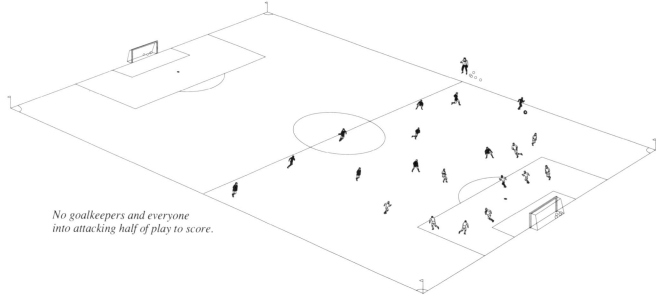

No goalkeepers and everyone into attacking half of play to score.

HEAD-A-GOAL

Teams from 9-a-side to 11-a-side. No goalkeepers. Only goals scored by "headers" count. Can be worked in conjunction with "everyone in attacking half," as above. The elimination of goalkeepers guarantees more heading duels.

Objective: To encourage use of width; crossed ball situations; frequent attacking and defensive heading situations.

APPLICABILITY	
6, 7 & 8's	✗
9, 10 & 11's	✗
12-15's	✔
16 +	✔

11-a-side

It has been argued the only way to improve team play is by playing and practising in 11 vs 11… that anything less than 11 vs 11 is unrealistic.

It is an interesting argument, but to produce total realism in 11 vs 11 play, an 11 vs 11 practise would need to include all the ingredients of competitive match play, including — points in the standings for a win or tie; or a trophy for the winning team; and, in the case of the pros, 40,000 people in the stands plus bonus money for the winning team!

Supposing all of these things could be accomplished by some magical formula, how would you concentrate on defensive heading in an 11 vs 11 game? If that was a weakness that had been identified and needed correcting, chances are there would only be a handful of high balls into the defensive end. Even then, players weak at heading could elect to run backwards out of a heading challenge and attempt to control the ball with the body or feet instead.

While 11-a-side play is not the perfect vehicle for team development, it can be extremely useful. For instance, it will help players to get a much clearer "picture" of the team requirements and of the roles of the individuals within the team framework.

APPLICABILITY	
6, 7 & 8's	✗
9, 10 & 11's	✗
12-15's	✔
16 +	✔

It is important in 11-a-side practise that coaches encourage the team to work at the strategies and patterns that have been agreed upon and practised. It is likely some parts will break down when put into the 11 vs 11 situation, and these problems can then be dealt with by adjustment and further development.

The STRENGTHS and LIMITATIONS of 11 vs 11 practise have been outlined above.

Many Ways Up Everest

Allan Brown, the former coach of Burnley, Sheffield Wednesday and Sunderland of the English Football League, used to say: "There are many ways up Everest!" He was referring to coaching methods and tactical formations. Allan Brown is so right.

Reaching the pinnacle of soccer has been accomplished in many different ways and not by just one training method. So, although there may be "many ways up Everest," we know some ways will mean a greater chance of success. Some routes are hazardous and could result in disaster.

Allan Brown is acknowledged as the "inventor" of Shadow Play. There are many coaches around the world, including myself, who had the privilege of studying under the "Master." We all use the "Shadow" method with our teams. Ironically, Allan Brown was criticized — by players and media — for his over-use of Shadow Play. What the players were saying is: "There are many ways up Everest, let's try some of them for a change!" And that is fair. Players need variety and fresh challenges. As coaches, we have to realize one practise system will not be enough and we have to develop a mixture, to give variety and balance to the training program.

But there is a happy medium. We are coaches, not "entertainers" — even though one important aim of every practise session is to try to make the session enjoyable.

Appendix

The Goalkeeper's Team Role

The goalkeeper is not some specialist freak. He is an important member of the team. If coaches ignore the goalkeepers, they do so at their own peril. At the same time, goalkeepers must not be allowed to think of themselves as "different" — otherwise they may ostracize themselves from teammates.

The goalkeeper plays an important tactical role by being the "eyes" of the team. From the back of the team, the goalkeeper can see all, and from that position can help direct play.

The goalkeeper should be encouraged to play a leadership role in communicating information to the team — in particular the defenders.

The goalkeeper should physically move up and back with the team as the ball moves up and down the field. Of course, the goalkeeper would not move out much further than the edge of the penalty box.

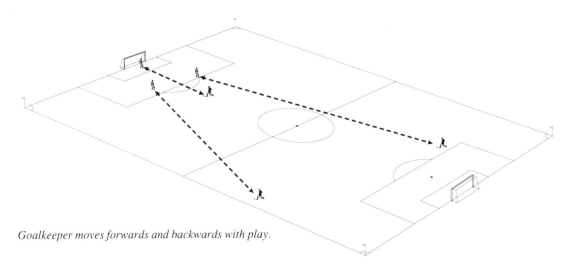

Goalkeeper moves forwards and backwards with play.

By moving up and back, the goalkeeper stays in contact with the field players, and is also better able to move out of the penalty area to clear a long "kick and hope" ball.

The coach must work with both the goalkeeper and the field players in certain key areas, where the goalkeeper's role assumes critical importance in the deployment of players. These "critical areas" are:

1. Defending at corners.
2. Defending at free kicks.
3. Defending at throw-ins.
4. Moving players out of defending positions after a clearance.
5. Instructing defenders about their positions, plus any adjustments required as the opposition builds an attack.
6. Informing teammates of the goalkeeper's intended actions, e.g., coming out for a cross ball or a through ball.

Goalkeeping practise should never be ignored by the coach. Also team goalkeeping must be an integral part of all collective defending and attacking practise.

FACTORS IN "TEAM DEVELOPMENT"

TEAM SHAPE

Positions & Numerical Arrangement of Players	Principles of Team Play Supporting play Use of width of field Offside

PHILOSOPHY AND ORGANIZATION

OFFENSE	DEFENSE	RE-START STRATEGY	OFFSIDE STRATEGY
Long/short ball mix Build up play through ⅓'s of field Attacks from flanks Attacks through middle	High pressure defense (near opponent's goal) Low pressure defense (retreating system) Marking system — Zone or man-marking	Defending & Attacking Throw-ins Free kicks Corner kicks Kick-offs Penalties Goal kicks	Influence on team shape Organization & strategy Fluid play Set plays

Coach's Questionnaire

This is a short questionnaire presented with the objective of getting you to think about the content of your practise sessions. It is not meant as an accurate indicator of your ability as a coach, nor as a rating of your practise sessions. These questions refer to actual preparation time spent working on "collective defending and attacking." Do not include in you estimates time spent in the end-of-session scrimmage if, during that time, the game is allowed to go "free."

1. **How often do you spend time in the practise session addressing the areas of collective team defending and attacking?**

    Never (   )   Occasionally (   )   Regularly (   )

2. **How much time (percentage of total time not including "free scrimmaging") do you spend in "collective team preparation?"**

    0 – 10% (   )   10 – 20% (   )   20 – 40% (   )   40% + (   )

3. **Of your total "team development" time, how much of it is given to "theory" (lectures, team talks, chalk talks) as opposed to practical work?**

    20% (   )   40% (   )   60% (   )

If you do not practise team play regularly . . .
If you spend less then 20% of practise time in "team" preparation . . .
If more than 20% of your team work is "theoretical" . . .
IT IS TIME TO RE-THINK YOUR PRACTISE PROGRAM.

Even if you are devoting a reasonable amount of time to the "team consideration,"
CAN THAT TIME BE USED MORE EFFECTIVELY?

As coaches we must always question ourselves, our methods, and the program we are running.

Sample Session Plan for U-16 Team

THEME: Team play — attacking support.
ANTICIPATED NUMBER OF PLAYERS: 16.
EQUIPMENT: Soccer field, marker disks, cones, poles, training vests and balls.
LENGTH OF SESSION: 90 minutes (including changeovers and water breaks).

INTRODUCTORY ACTIVITY

SHADOW PLAY

1. 11 vs 5 — gradual warm-up. Easy jogging, with 2 touch rule — no passes over 15 yards. No long crosses. Side-foot shots only. Three sets of 2 minutes of Shadow Play, each followed by 1 minute of stretching.   9 minutes

2. Increase speed of running (fast jog) — also increase length of passes. Three minutes + 1 minute stretching.   4 minutes

3. All-out play — no "conditions" plus normal short and long passing, crossing, running and sprinting.   3 minutes

4. Finale — 1 touch play only.   4 minutes

5 vs 2

2 groups of 8 players — 20 x 20 yards area.   10 minutes

4-GOAL GAME

8 vs 8 — 40 x 40 yards area.   20 minutes

8 vs 8 SCRIMMAGE

Half field. Free play.   25 minutes

SPRINTING COMPETITION

10 short sprints (varying between 6 – 18 yards). Everyone together — winners/losers identified.   5 minutes

GOALKEEPERS

During the 5 vs 2 and the 4-Goal Game, it's a good opportunity for the goalkeepers to work on some aspect of goalkeeping, e.g., shot stopping, either on their own or with an assistant coach.